Battleground Britain

MARSTON MOOR

ENGLISH CIVIL WAR
– JULY 1644

Battleground Britain

MARSTON MOOR

ENGLISH CIVIL WAR
– JULY 1644

David Clark

LEO COOPER

First published in 2004
by LEO COOPER
an imprint of
Pen & Sword Books Ltd
47 Church Street, Barnsley, South Yorkshire, S70 2AS

Copyright © David Clark 2004
Landscape photographs by David Clark, © 2004

ISBN 0 85052 985 9

A CIP catalogue of this book is available
from the British Library

Printed by CPI UK

CONTENTS

Preface

Writing in *The History of the Rebellion and Civil Wars in England*, the Earl of Clarendon remarks that 'there were more sharp skirmishes and more notable battles in that one county of York, than in all the kingdom besides.' In fact, Clarendon's observation could be taken in a wider context, for Yorkshire had already won a reputation as the scene of several memorable encounters prior to the era of the English Civil War.

Many a bloody contest, unrecorded for posterity, must have taken place within 'Yorkshire' long before the formation of the administrative unit of that name. Doubtless, there were confrontations during the Roman occupation, between Rome's legions and the warlike Brigantes who occupied northern Britain. In AD 122, for example, the Ninth Legion, based at York, simply disappeared from recorded history. The only possible solution to the mystery is that it was routed and wiped out in a great battle.

The first major recorded 'Yorkshire' battle is mentioned by Bede in *A History of the English Church and People*. This was the Battle of 'Heathfield' (present-day Hatfield) at which Edwin, the first Christian king of Northumbria, was slain by Penda, the heathen king of Mercia. Bede goes on to describe the Battle of Winwoed (near Scholes) in AD

Some Yorkshire battlefields do remain essentially unchanged over time. Barrett's sketch (c.1896) of 'The Shallows' at Stamford Bridge is not dissimilar to the scene today.

655, where Edwin's brother, Oswy, gained revenge by defeating Penda's pagan hordes.

One of Yorkshire's most celebrated battles took place a millennium later, in 1066 at Stamford Bridge, where King Harold destroyed Hardrada's Norwegian invaders, before marching to his own doom at Hastings. In 1322, the rebellion of Thomas, Earl of Lancaster against Edward II was quelled at the Battle of Boroughbridge. At Wakefield in 1460, the Red Rose of Lancaster triumphed over the House of York, only to be trampled underfoot three months later, at the Battle of Towton – with up to 60,000 participants, the largest battle ever fought on British soil.

In addition, throughout the Middle Ages, Yorkshire was a target for marauding bands of Scots. In 1138, the army of King David was repulsed by the English at the Battle of the Standard near Northallerton. At Myton, in 1319, the Scots were victorious in the famous 'White Battle', so called because the English dead included over two hundred monks, their white habits steeped in blood. And at the Battle of Byland in 1322, the army of Edward II was destroyed by Robert the Bruce, the Scots going on to pillage and plunder the countryside as far south as Beverley.

Of course, as Yorkshire covers such a large area, it might be considered unusual if a number of battles had not been fought within its confines. Also, much of Ermine Street, the longest and most important of the roads constructed by the Romans, developed into the Great North Road, which retains its importance to this day, and it is no coincidence that Yorkshire battlefields display a tendency to cling to this prince of thoroughfares. If rival armies were marching towards a confrontation in Yorkshire, the chances were that they would meet at some point on or beside the Great North Road. However, to suggest that more battles occurred in Yorkshire than in any other county for purely geographical reasons would be to ignore the political significance of the county in bygone days.

There was a time when York rivalled London in terms of importance. It was from York that Edwin, who lost his life at Heathfield, ruled his kingdom of Northumbria.

Sandal – December, 1460.

A number of battlefields in Yorkshire are marked by memorials. At Towton, for example, a cross erected in 1928 commemorated the battle of 1461 while, at Wakefield, a Victorian memorial marks the spot where, a year earlier, the Duke of York died fighting for the cause of the white rose.

Towton – March 1461.

Examples of military dress during the Civil War period as depicted by a Victorian artist.

William the Conqueror saw fit to fortify the settlement as a base for controlling the unruly North, and it would grow to become the second largest city in England and the regional capital. Richard III, too, was careful to court the city of York in his quest to secure his position as 'Lord of the North.' And it was to York that Charles I would repair when he abandoned London in 1642.

It was inevitable, therefore, that the Civil War would add to Yorkshire's battlefield pedigree. If not especially well known, most Yorkshire Civil War battlefields are relatively unspoiled. Those which stood in open country, such as Adwalton and Seacroft Moor, still do so. Even those which lay in urban landscapes, such as Selby and Tadcaster, remain largely unchanged in terms of surviving street patterns. The best preserved, befitting its importance, is

Marston Moor, arguably the decisive battle of the Civil War, and certainly the most widely known. Here, with the help of contemporary accounts, it is possible to follow, literally step by step, the course of this fateful encounter.

Site exploration is important because it is by visiting the ground once trodden by kings and would-be kings that we can begin to experience more fully a sense of identity with the past. Half-formed images of battles which have shaped history spring to life as we stand on hilltops or in broad pastures where crowns were won and lost. The Civil War redefined the roles of the monarchy and parliament, and the battlefields upon which the major issues were decided are of no less historical importance than many an ancient building which is protected by law. Unfortunately, battlefields do not include any standing remains, unless it be the occasional memorial, and it becomes more difficult, therefore, to produce an argument for the preservation of specific sites.

A battlefield explored is no longer simply a name on a map – and exploration is very properly an integral part of the 'Battleground' series. It follows that this book comprises two sections. In the first part, a sketch of the Civil War in Yorkshire is followed by a description of the Marston Moor campaign, the battle itself and its results. The second part is essentially a hands-on guide to an exploration of the battlefield and sites of related interest. The terms 'Cavalier' and 'Roundhead' have been used throughout to denote the forces of King and Parliament respectively, on the grounds that they are labels with which most people are comfortable and which add a touch of colour to what was, after all, one of the most colourful episodes in English history. As a long-standing devotee of the *Battleground Europe* series, I find it particularly gratifying to be able to contribute to such an exciting new venture as *Battleground Britain*.

DAVID CLARK
October 2003

Chapter 1

THE CIVIL WAR IN YORKSHIRE

Prior to the Battle of Marston Moor in 1644, a Roundhead officer was riding through the village of Long Marston when he came across a farmer. Reining in his horse, he posed the question: 'Have you seen any of the King's soldiers – and who are you for, King or Parliament?' The countryman replied, 'What! be them two fall'n out, then?'

The man was called Richard Wright – or so his descendants claim – and, although apocryphal, the tale does serve to suggest that, despite two years of civil war, no battle sufficiently substantial to engage public attention had yet taken place in the largest county in England. It also reminds us that Yorkshire folk then, as now, were of a distinctly parochial turn of mind, being relatively unmoved by the political and religious radicalism of the time. Indeed, in 1642, as the rift between Charles I and Parliament widened, it was hoped that matters could be resolved elsewhere and that Yorkshire could stand aloof. Yet, from January of that year, Yorkshire Cavaliers and Roundheads were making preliminary preparations for war.

The pattern of support for both sides did not follow hard and fast lines. Generally speaking, however, the poorer, conservative rural areas declared for the King, while the prosperous commercial towns supported Parliament. The rustics had little choice in the matter, usually following blindly in the wake of their landlords. More volatile was the situation in urban areas, where the acquisition of wealth was dependent upon a combination of industry and economic stability, as opposed to privilege. Some businesses, such as iron working, leather working, shipbuilding, lead and coal mining, would derive the usual benefits accruing from a war economy. Other entrepreneurs, less sanguine in their expectations, were prepared to back the side most likely to win or to take the course of action which promised the least disruption to everyday business.

In Hull, for example, several of the leading citizens were 'famous king's-men', but their priority was 'to keep the town in peace and safety'. When Sir John Hotham, for Parliament, appeared at the gates of Hull on 14 January 1642, he was rebuffed by the lord mayor, only to be admitted a few days later when the latter submitted to threats. Hull became the first town to be seized by Parliament – and a most important acquisition it turned out to be, not least because of its mighty arsenal which comprised the better part of 120 field pieces, 20,000 arms and 7,000 barrels of gunpowder.

Certainly, the King overestimated the extent of his subjects' affection for him – particularly in Yorkshire. While Charles was staying in York, the Cavalier and diarist, Sir Henry Slingsby, was ordered 'to take 20 of a company to do the duty of a soldier and be a guard to the King's person'. Slingsby records that he 'perceived a great backwardness in them; and upon Summons few or none appeared.' A subsequent fund-raising meeting on Heworth Moor 'produced nothing else but a confused murmer and noise, as at an Election... some crying [for] the King, some [for] the Parliament.' Many prospective supporters, like Slingsby himself, who lobbied long and hard for commissions, were told that they would be granted only if each recipient undertook to equip a body of men at his own expense.

The man appointed by Parliament to attend to the overall defence of Yorkshire was Ferdinando, Lord Fairfax. Described by his irascible father as 'a mere coward', any reputation he subsequently acquired as a commander was destined to be eclipsed by that of his own son, Sir Thomas. The Fairfaxes had hoped for a peaceful solution to the nation's ills and, when he left York, Charles had no reason to doubt their loyalty.

Initially leading the Yorkshire Cavaliers was Henry Clifford, Earl of Cumberland. Even his friends

In September 1642, Ferdinando, 2nd Lord Fairfax, was appointed commander of the Parliamentary army in Yorkshire and was largely successful in keeping in check the superior forces of the Marquis of Newcastle

recognised that 'his genius was not military', and he was soon replaced by William Cavendish, Earl of Newcastle, one of the wealthiest landowners in the kingdom. Already responsible for Northumberland, Durham, Cumberland and Westmoreland, Newcastle was loathe to take on additional responsibilities. He was expected to outfit and maintain his own men, and although some thought he could well afford it, he demanded financial guarantees before venturing forth. Apparently satisfied, he marched from Northumberland to York, overrunning en route, at Piercebridge, a small Roundhead force led by Captain John Hotham, son of Sir John on 1 December 1642. On his arrival in York, the governor, Sir Thomas Glemham, a committed Cavalier, presented him with the keys of the city.

Most of the fighting in Yorkshire took place in the West Riding, where the Fairfaxes enjoyed widespread support in the clothing towns. The first battle took place at Bradford in October 1642, Sir Thomas Fairfax reporting that his poorly armed force of 300 men bravely repelled an assault by some 700 Cavaliers.

A few weeks later, at Wetherby, Sir Thomas was surprised by an assault force out of York, led by Sir Thomas Glemham. According to the Cavaliers, who attacked at 6.00 am, Fairfax was still putting on his boots when the attack came, although Fairfax claimed he was already astride his horse. Rousing his troops, he repelled two assaults and Glemham was eventually beaten back.

Sir Henry Slingsby, in providing an account of this action, describes a particular incident between

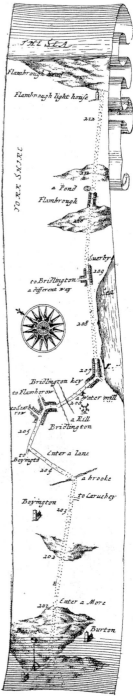

In the seventeenth century, several road maps in scroll form were produced for the use of travellers. Mileage was indicated as were beacons, gibbets, brooks, bridges, churches, mills, moors and commons. The illustration, from a map, produced in 1675 by John Ogilby, depicts Bridlington on the East Yorkshire coast. Even today, this style of mapping is preferred by some ramblers and cyclists.

Bridges were the focal points of many battles and skirmishes in the Civil War in Yorkshire. The bridge spanning the River Wharfe at Wetherby was of particular significance owing to its proximity to York.

a Roundhead, Captain Atkinson, and a Cavalier, Lieutenant Colonel Norton. Atkinson, on horseback, shot at – and missed – Norton as he entered the town. Norton dragged Atkinson from his mount as troops from both sides approached to give aid. Norton was beaten into a ditch while Atkinson suffered repeated blows which broke his thigh, 'of which wound he died'. Slingsby describes the altercation as 'A sore scuffle between two that had been neighbours and intimate friends.' The action was only a skirmish, with a handful of casualties on both sides, but it encapsulates the tragic nature of the conflict.

Sir Thomas Fairfax excelled in such small scale cut-and-thrust affairs, mounting his own guerrilla raids, closely fought encounters within the confines of narrow cobbled streets. With rarely more than a few hundred men under their command, it was not open to the Fairfaxes to do much more. Towards the end of 1642, when Newcastle arrived on the scene with 6,000 troops, they retreated to Tadcaster where, in a fight which raged throughout the afternoon of 7 December, they successfully defended the bridge spanning the River Wharfe.

Short of ammunition, the Fairfaxes had to abandon Tadcaster and fell back on Selby, cutting themselves off from the West

Riding. A week later, resolved to take the fight to the enemy, Sir Thomas raided Sherburn-in-Elmet which was held by the Cavaliers. In a typical piece of derring-do, he led his men in a charge along the barricaded main street and had his horse shot from under him before the defenders were put to flight. Cavalier reinforcements forced an orderly retreat to Selby yet, as a result of this minor success, Fairfax later recalled that 'we lay more quietly by them [the Cavaliers] a good while after.'

In fact, Newcastle was making efforts to secure Leeds, Wakefield and Bradford. In so doing, he was compelled to divide his army. Leeds and Wakefield were occupied and plundered, but Bradford proved a more stubborn nut to crack. On 18 December, Newcastle attacked the town, but met with fierce resistance from apprentice boys armed with a motley assortment of weapons, including fowling-pieces, clubs and scythes, who set up barricades and withstood an artillery barrage. In savage hand-to-hand fighting, the Cavalier assault was repulsed. Here was a town which it seemed the Roundheads could hold, and Sir Thomas was

A string of Yorkshire castles held by the Cavaliers formed a precious lifeline for their cause. One of the strongest was Pontefract Castle, the last Royalist stronghold in England to fall.

despatched to lend support, being 'received with great joy and acclamation of the country'.

Despite successfully defending Bradford from several more attacks, Sir Thomas, disdaining to 'lie idle', decided to launch an attack on Leeds. On 23 January 1643, having received a negative response to his summons to surrender, Fairfax stormed the barricades and fought his way into the streets. In the face of such a resolute assault, many of the defenders 'cast down their arms, and rendered themselves prisoners.' Also captured was a 'good store of ammunition.' Newcastle, who had established temporary headquarters at Pontefract, withdrew to York. Unfortunately, with limited manpower, the Roundhead army was unable to consolidate yet another success, and had no course but to continue its nomadic existence, moving from town to town as the occasion demanded.

Newcastle himself was preoccupied with weightier matters. In February 1643, Queen Henrietta Maria arrived in Bridlington, accompanied by 1,000 mercenaries, a considerable quantity of arms and ammunition and £80,000 in cash – the result of several months spent on the Continent canvassing for support. The Queen's safety became Newcastle's top priority and he marched forty miles to the small fishing port in order to escort her safely to York.

Henrietta Maria's arrival was no secret. Captain John Hotham rode up from Hull to inform Newcastle that he and his father were prepared to change sides for a price – £20,000 to be exact. Newcastle left the matter open while winning an undertaking from Hotham that the Queen would not be molested en route to York. Her convoy of 500 wagons trundled across the Yorkshire Wolds unhindered, to Burton Fleming, Malton and finally York, where she arrived safely on 8 March.

Henrietta Maria was to remain in York for three months, creating a difficult situation for Newcastle who had to afford her the deference demanded by her position while striving to retain his authority in military matters. Her visitors included the Earl of Montrose who needed 'the king's warrant' to help him bring to fruition plans for a rising in Scotland in support of Charles. Montrose also warned of the likelihood of a Scottish invasion in support of the Roundheads – an idea which was given little credence. By the time Charles gave Montrose his official blessing, in February 1644, Leven's army was already across the

Lacking the facilities afforded by a major east coast port, Queen Henrietta Maria, arriving with men and arms from the Continent, was forced to put into Bridlington, where she was reduced to hiding in a ditch.

border. Another guest at the King's Manor was Sir Hugh Cholmley, Roundhead governor of Scarborough, who arrived in disguise, with a black patch over one eye. Like the Hothams, he was considering changing his allegiance. Despite his piratical posturing, his intentions were sincere for, less than a week later, while the Hothams wavered, Cholmley announced that, henceforth, he would be holding Scarborough for the King.

With the Queen secure, Newcastle was free to resume his pursuit of the Fairfaxes. Thus, at the end of March 1643, in the course of his enforced perambulations, Lord Fairfax, marching from Selby to Leeds, found that Newcastle was once more hot on his trail. In an effort to draw off the Cavalier army, Sir Thomas attacked Tadcaster. Although it bought his father valuable time, he himself was caught out in the open five miles from Leeds, on Seacroft Moor. Unable to rally his men, Fairfax watched while the cavalry of Lord Goring destroyed his force. It was only with some difficulty that he managed to reach the relative safety of Leeds. As he himself put it, 'This was one of the greatest losses we ever received.'

From Leeds, Fairfax was sent once more to Bradford from which base, with the approval of his father, he attacked Cavalier

17

held Wakefield on 21 May. A typically pugnacious assault carried the day, with the now familiar pattern of Roundhead cavalry mowing down Cavalier infantry in the streets. Fairfax was also developing an imprudent habit. Not for the first time – nor the last – he got so far ahead of his own men that he lost contact with them. Approached by two enemy officers, he saw:

> '...a place in the Work where men used to go over... and made my horse leap over... And so, by a good Providence, got to my men again.'

Aside from stores of ammunition, Fairfax acquired nearly 1,500 prisoners which he was able to exchange for the Roundhead prisoners taken at Seacroft Moor, most of whom he describes as local rustics 'whose wives and children were... importunate for their release.'

This reversal of fortune was both compounded and assuaged by the departure from York on 4 June of Henrietta Maria who set out for Oxford to join the king. Newcastle was bound to provide an escort for her, but at least the self-styled 'Her She Majesty Generalissima' ceased to be his responsibility.

Having been frustrated for nearly two years by a much inferior force, Newcastle now resolved to bring matters to a head by seeking out the Roundheads, whether they be at Leeds or Bradford. They were, in fact, at Bradford. The Fairfaxes decided to march out of the town and meet the Cavaliers on open ground. On the morning of 30 June, the two armies met on Adwalton Moor, about five miles to the south east of Bradford.

The Fairfaxes had planned to start out no later than 4.00 am, but did not get under way until nearer 8.00 am. They had marched just four miles when they came upon the enemy. Sir Thomas suspected treachery for the Cavaliers were ready and waiting for them, 'drawn up in Battalia' – the main body of infantry flanked on either side by cavalry – on broken ground by the village of Adwalton. The Cavalier army which, according to Sir Thomas, was 10,000 to 12,000 strong probably numbered no more than 9,000. Sir Thomas put the Roundhead force at 3,000 men, and although Newcastle found its strength greater than he had expected, the Cavaliers certainly held the advantage, as many of the Roundheads were untrained 'clubmen'. Yet, the force did include a high proportion of musketeers, ideal for the terrain. Newcastle's army was deployed over open ground, his left wing hampered somewhat by open-cast coal mines.

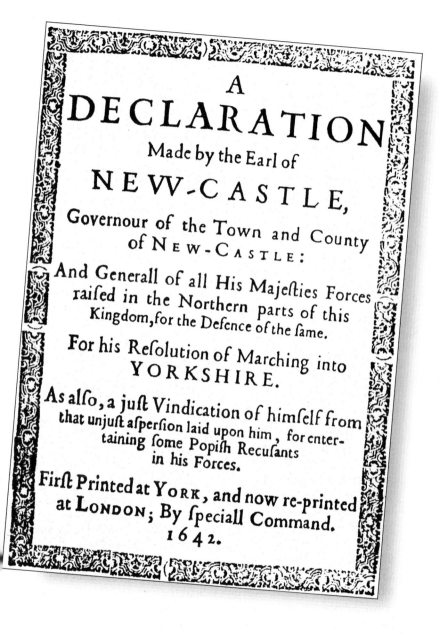

A DECLARATION

Made by the Earl of

NEW-CASTLE,

Governour of the Town and County
of NEW-CASTLE:

And Generall of all His Majesties Forces
raised in the Northern parts of this
Kingdom, for the Defence of the same.

For his Resolution of Marching into
YORKSHIRE.

As also, a just Vindication of himself from
that unjust aspersion laid upon him, for entertaining some Popish Recusants
in his Forces.

First Printed at YORK, and now re-printed
at LONDON; By speciall Command.
1642.

*Title page of a pamphlet published by the then Earl of Newcastle in which
he sets out his reasons for marching into Yorkshire.*

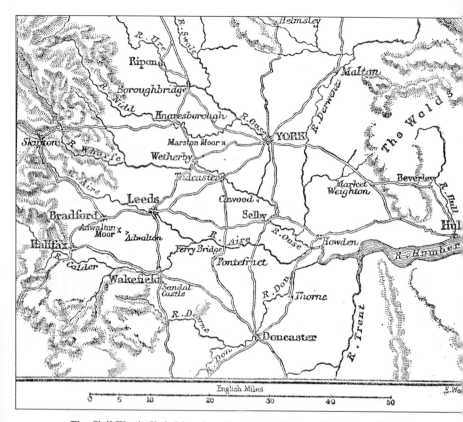

The Civil War in Yorkshire, from Gardiner's History of the Great Civil War.

Roundhead mobility was compromised by a number of enclosures and an undulating landscape which meant that Sir Thomas on the right wing was unable to see what might be happening on the left. Two Cavalier cavalry charges were beaten off by Sir Thomas, the Cavalier commanders, Colonels Howard and Herne both losing their lives. The Roundhead cavalry on the left, together with the infantry pressed forward with such effect that the Cavaliers appeared to be on the verge of collapse. At this point, a furious counter-charge on the Roundhead left, led by Colonel Skirton, 'a wild and desperate man', achieved a breakthrough, putting the Roundheads to flight. On the other wing, Newcastle personally led a charge 'into the very rage of the battle', dispersing Sir Thomas's cavalry. It seems that, once again, Sir Thomas had pressed too far forward, for Newcastle got in behind him, cutting off the retreat to Bradford. Thus, while the road to Bradford remained open to his father, Sir Thomas himself initially had to flee south to Halifax. On that day, up to 500 Roundheads died and 1,400 were taken prisoner.

Lord Fairfax ultimately moved on to Leeds while Sir Thomas, of necessity, made his way to Bradford by a circuitous route. He organised a makeshift defence of the town, during which the exterior of the tower of the parish church was protected with wool-packs. The position seemed hopeless and in the early hours of 2 July 1643, Bradford was evacuated to the cry of 'every man for himself'. It was also a case of every woman for herself, for Sir Thomas's wife, Lady Anne, fell into Newcastle's hands. After a few days, Newcastle put her in his own coach and sent her on to her husband. It was a generous gesture, in

The Earl of Newcastle.

keeping with the fast disappearing traditions of medieval chivalry.

The Cavaliers now held Yorkshire with the one very significant exception of Hull. Even here, they came within a hair's breadth of gaining control. Sir John Hotham's plans to defect had been uncovered just in time and he and his son had been arrested. Thus, it remained a Roundhead stronghold to which the Fairfaxes were able to retreat. Yet, with Newcastle's campaign apparently all but concluded, the King wrote to him to enquire what he now meant to do with his army. Charles wanted him to march south as part of a co-ordinated plan to take London, but Newcastle was worried about the risk of leaving an unfriendly Hull to his rear. It seemed a better idea to subdue Hull first and so, on 2 September 1643, he embarked upon a siege, beginning painstaking work on a series of extensive earthworks, 'at least half a mile in length, with strong forts, half moons and breastworks, slanting nearer and nearer towards the town.'

Newcastle also commandeered all foodstuffs from the surrounding countryside and cut off the city's fresh water supply. In return, Lord Fairfax, newly appointed as Governor of Hull, ordered the Humber's banks to be cut, flooding the land 'for two miles about'. A combination of high tides and heavy rains ensured that the besiegers endured thoroughly miserable conditions, prompting a commentator to note 'that those without the town seemed likelier to rot than those within to starve.'

In fact, only rarely was any Civil War siege effective in terms of bottling up a garrison. In the case of Hull, reinforcements and supplies could – and did – come in from the sea and from Lincolnshire, via the River Humber. On 11 October, Newcastle committed 4,000 troops to an all-out assault. Despite coming under extremely heavy fire, they came within a pistol-shot of success when the garrison counter-attacked, compelling them to retreat. To add to Newcastle's woes, he received news that earlier in the day, Cavalier forces in Lincolnshire had been defeated at the Battle of Winceby. To add insult to injury, he learned that Sir Thomas Fairfax had been present at the fight, having slipped across the Humber with his cavalry some weeks earlier. With the approach of winter and the traditional end of the campaigning season, Newcastle despaired of ever taking Hull. That night, he took the decision to withdraw to York immediately.

Had the King's grand plan to attack London in the autumn materialised, events might have taken a very different turn. Instead, the Cavaliers, masters of Yorkshire, went on to the defensive. Nevertheless, on 27 October, in recompense for his efforts on the King's behalf, Newcastle was created Marquis of Newcastle.

And there, as far as Yorkshire was concerned, matters rested for the remainder of the year as both sides settled themselves into winter quarters. Sporadic fighting continued in adjacent counties. Sir Thomas Fairfax, temporarily exiled in Lincolnshire, fought at Lincoln and Gainsborough before making a foray into Cheshire. By this time, his men were in rags and he himself had to meet the cost of new uniforms. Newcastle, surrounded by his army, managed to spend Christmas at his Nottinghamshire home, Welbeck Abbey. He must have thought that little fighting of any consequence, necessitating the movement and supply of large armies, would occur until the following spring. However, on 19 January 1644, to his great alarm, a Scottish army, 20,000 strong, tramped through the snow to Berwick and crossed the border in support of the Roundhead cause.

Chapter 2

THE SIEGE OF YORK

he intervention of the Scots had been on the cards since 25 September 1643 when the English Parliament committed itself to what was known as the 'Solemn League and Covenant', through which it was agreed that Presbyterianism would be enforced in England and Wales. At least, this was the Scottish intention, but the proliferation of Protestant sects within the parliamentarian fold meant that implementation would be very difficult, if not impossible. Cunningly, therefore, the English contrived to introduce wording which, as far as they were concerned, left the matter open to interpretation. For the moment, the Roundheads' priority was to bring the Scots into the war on their side.

Regardless of the politics of the situation, Newcastle was now confronted by a serious problem. His own army had gradually been whittled down to 5,000 foot and 3,000 horse which he quickly mustered to march north in order to protect the town bearing his name. He left York in the care of Sir John Bellasis, commanding a garrison of 4,000 men. So swift was the Earl's progress that he reached Newcastle before the Scots, on 2 February 1644. In preparation for a siege, he burnt the northern suburbs of the town, Instead of marching in to Newcastle, all the invaders – commanded by Alexander Leslie, Earl of Leven – could do was to dig in.

Back in Yorkshire, the Fairfaxes were again on the prowl on their home turf. Early in April, Sir Thomas joined forces with his father at Ferrybridge, to make, according to Lord Fairfax, a combined force of 'Two thousand Horse and Dragoons, and Two thousand Foot'. Learning that Sir Thomas had been ordered north to lend support to the Scots, Bellasis, rather unwisely, led 1,500 cavalry and 1,800 foot soldiers out of York in an attempt to stop him.

On 11 April, the two forces met at Selby. Bellasis lay within the town which the Roundheads stormed, 'with the Foot in three divisions, one led by my self, a seconde by Sir John Meldrum, and a third by Lieutenant Colonel Needham'. The Cavalier defences

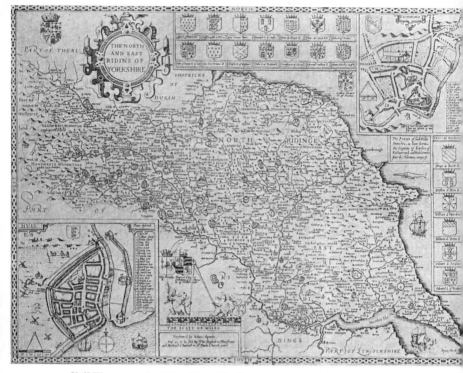

Civil War generals did not have the luxury of maps of the calibre of Ogilby's. Map making was in a period of transition, somewhere between an art form and an exact science – hence while John Speed's map of the North and East Ridings of Yorkshire (1610) does show rivers, towns and villages, roads are ignored.

held for two hours. Lord Fairfax states that he broke the stalemate, his own regiment forcing 'a passage by the River side'. This conflicts with Sir Thomas's account: 'I getting a Barricado open, which let us betwixt the houses and the river.' What is clear is that, once again, Sir Thomas got too far ahead of his men:

> 'Other Horse came up, and charged us again, where my horse was overthrown; being single a little before my men; who presently relieved me.'

The Cavaliers were put to flight. A wounded Bellasis – cousin to Sir Thomas – was taken prisoner together with most of his infantry and, concludes Lord Fairfax,

> 'the Enemy was wholly routed, and as many as could saved themselves by flight, some towards Cawood, some towards Pontefract, and the rest towards York.'

On receipt of this catastrophic news, Newcastle broke off hostilities with Leven and made a forced march south to save beleaguered York. So unobtrusive was his departure, in the early hours of 13 April, that Leven was unaware of it for several hours. By the following morning, the Scots were hot on the trail, catching up with Newcastle's rearguard at Darlington, capturing supplies that he could ill afford to lose. On 16 April, Newcastle reached York, with Leven having given up the chase in favour of linking up with the Fairfaxes.

Newcastle was greeted by an anxious garrison 500 strong. The city itself was protected by stout medieval stone walls, outside of which, in turn, was a moat. Entrance was effected principally via a number of gates: Walmgate, Micklegate, Bootham Bar and Monk Bar. Integrated into the system was a Norman castle, Clifford's Tower. Although potentially daunting, the defences had been long neglected and not until the outbreak of the Civil War had restoration work begun. Clifford's Tower was strengthened and repairs made to the walls, barricades were erected in the narrow streets and gun emplacements constructed at strategic positions.

On 18 April 1644, Leven and the Fairfaxes met at Wetherby, creating a joint force totalling 4,000 cavalry and 16,000 infantry. Scottish desertions had thinned Leven's ranks, but the combined army outnumbered that of the Cavaliers by three to one. The allied commanders were well aware of the vagaries of siege warfare. They had insufficient men to put a stranglehold on York and there was always the risk that Newcastle would mount counter-attacks – not to mention the ever-present danger of being subjected to a flank assault by a Cavalier relief force. The decision was taken to concentrate their army to the south of the city.

Another logistical problem for the allies concerned the absence of a bridge across the River Ouse outside the city, so pontoon bridges were organised at Acaster Malbis and at Cawood.

Newcastle did manage to evacuate most of his cavalry. The decision to do so reduced his capacity to harass the allies but, as well as saving on fodder, he hoped that they could be made better use of elsewhere. He had also written to the King, begging that 'some speedy course is taken to give us relief'. There was no immediate urgency as far as supplies were concerned, yet the requirements of Newcastle's 4,000 infantry and the civilian population would eventually place a strain on resources. All provisions were sequestered, placed in a central storehouse and distributed on the basis that everyone would be rationed to one

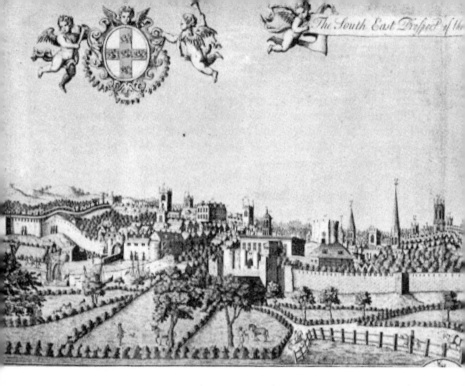

meal per day. Up to four soldiers might be billeted in a house, free of charge.

To inspire loyalty, Newcastle made everyone take an oath. All had to swear that they:

> *'beare true faith, and Allegiance to His Sacred Majestie, and his Crowne; and to my might and power will assist him, his Generalls and all under their command, against all such as have taken or shall take up Armes against him...'*

The Roundheads would not have disagreed with this, for it was their contention that they too represented the King's interests. The parting of the ways came with the concluding portion of the oath, relating to Leven's army, which required the individual:

> *'to the utmost of mine abilitie with the hazard of my life, and fortunes, assist his Majestie, his Gènèralls, and all under their Commands, in resisting, opposing and pursuing such Scots, in a hostile way, as rebells, and traytors against his Majestie, and enemies to the Crowne of England.'*

In the early days of the siege, the Fairfaxes took full advantage of Newcastle's impotence by reducing neighbouring Cavalier strongholds, including Stamford Bridge, Wakefield's Sandal Castle and several fortified manor houses. Leven established his

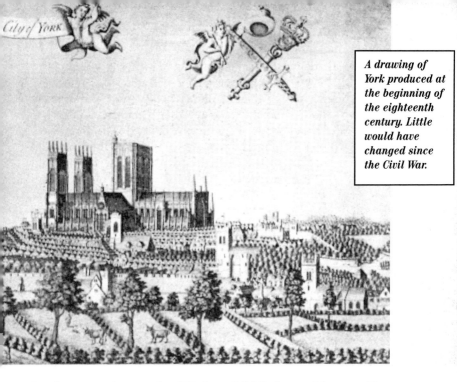

A drawing of York produced at the beginning of the eighteenth century. Little would have changed since the Civil War.

headquarters due south of York, at Middlethorpe Manor, with a view to investing York to the west as far as Poppleton. Lord Fairfax, with his headquarters at Heslington Hall, covered the eastern approaches to the city between Middlethorpe and the River Foss.

In reality, of course, both sides were tied down and the crucial question was, who would be riding to the rescue. Newcastle's likely saviour was the King's nephew, Prince Rupert of the Rhine. Rupert's mother was Charles' sister, Elizabeth who had married Frederick V, Elector Palatine of the Rhine and, although only twenty-two at the outbreak of the Civil War, Rupert was already a veteran of several European campaigns. His official title was 'General of the Horse' but his privileged position as kinsman to the King could lead to difficulties where issues of rank were involved – as Newcastle would discover. For the time being, however, Rupert symbolised salvation.

Allied hopes centred on the Earl of Manchester. General of the Army of the Eastern Association, Manchester had accompanied the young Charles to Spain in 1623, in a plan to acquire the Infanta as a wife. At Charles' coronation, he was made a Knight of the Bath and yet, by 1642, relations between courtier and monarch had deteriorated to such an extent that Manchester was accused of treason along with Pym, Hampden, Haselrige, Holles and Strode, in the warrant which the King tried to serve in the House of Commons on 4 January. Like Newcastle – and just as unfairly – he was often described as lethargic and ill fitted to be a soldier.

By the middle of May, stories were circulating to the effect that Rupert was on his way to raise the siege. Actually, he was tied down in Oxfordshire, where the Roundhead army of the Earl of Essex was threatening Oxford. While the Cavaliers may have considered it advisable to encourage misleading rumours, they succeeded only in stirring the Earl of Manchester into action. Suspending operations in Lincolnshire, he proceeded to York with an army of 6,000 foot and 3,000 horse. On 24 May, he was at Gainsborough and by 27 May, had reached Thorne, near Doncaster, from where he advanced to Selby and then on to York. On 3 June, his troops finally assumed positions to plug the gap to the north of the city.

Manchester's progress had been steady – some would say tardy – but he was a careful commander who always ensured that his men were both well disciplined and well provisioned. Both Leven and the Fairfaxes borrowed supplies from him. That Manchester was slow in getting his men into place is testified to by an impatient Sir Thomas who remarks that after Manchester's arrival on the scene, 'the north side still remained open to the town' and that 'Some time was spent here without any considerable action'. Manchester did put in place a third pontoon bridge at Poppleton and eventually completed the encirclement of York by plugging the gap between the Ouse and the Foss.

There were now three armies investing York, a total of around 30,000 men yet, despite the allies' overwhelming numerical superiority, there was to be no mass onslaught. A battery was set up on Lamel Hill outside Walmgate Bar and, not without difficulty, a giant cannon called 'The Queen's Pocket Pistol', mounted upon it. One of a pair, firing shot weighing 85lbs (15.8kg), this gun had originally been in Newcastle's possession, but had been captured at the Siege of Hull. The suburbs outside Walmgate were also occupied and another battery erected at St Lawrence's Church.

The line of 'circumvallation' decided upon by the allies was quite unwieldy. At Gloucester (10 August – 5 September 1643), the besieging Cavaliers had set up a series of camps and batteries just 500 yards from the town; at Hull, to the west of the city, they had established an earthwork at Gallows Shore, very close to the walls. Here, at York, the Roundheads were content to remain at distances, to the south and south west, of up to a mile and a half.

To an extent, they were pinned back by a number of earthworks which lay outside the walls as a first line of defence. To the west lay three such defensive forts, all of which may have been in place before the siege. One of these, 'The Mount', was situated half a mile beyond Walmgate Bar; a second stood on Bishopthorpe Road and a third (probably) on Holgate Hill. On 7 June, the Scots attacked and occupied the latter two. The fort on 'The Mount' was saved by a relief party which sallied forth from the city.

As the allies crept closer, Newcastle tried to deprive them of cover by firing the suburbs, 'a lamentable fire in those places, most dolefull and dreadfull to many of us, who with sad hearts saw that fearfull fruit of wasting wars.' One potential arsonist was caught on the job within the Earl of Manchester's zone. Wearing a red coat, 'he had pitch, flax and other materials upon him for the fiering of the suburbs there, as yet free from the wasting flames.'

Newcastle also entered into a dialogue with the allies, creating the impression that he was prepared to consider terms of surrender. They took the bait and on 9 June 'reported their readiness to treate about the surrendering of the Citty in such sort, that mens lives and estates might not bee exposed to ruine'. Seizing upon one of their conditions for peace talks, that there should be 'no Cessation of Armes in any part of the Citty, but the places appointed for the Treaty', Newcastle declined. Despite receiving an ultimatum to surrender 'within the space of 24 houres', he stood firm and the allies agreed to a temporary general cease fire.

Representatives of the two sides met in the afternoon of 15 June in a tent 'set up for them betwixt two Forts, one of ours, lately taken from them, and one of theirs', thus placing the site in the general vicinity of 'The Mount'. Newcastle made the outlandish proposal that the garrison should be allowed 20 days' grace to give Prince Rupert an opportunity to come to its relief. Should no relief arrive, then the troops should be permitted to march out with everything they could carry and receive safe passage to a friendly garrison. Most provocatively, as far as the Scots were concerned, Newcastle insisted that 'no Oath, Covenant, or

Protestation be administered'. In their rejection of these terms, the allies proposed that Newcastle's 'common souldiers shall have free liberty and licence to depart and go to their homes, and to carry with them their clothes and their own money' while his officers 'shall have liberty to go to their own homes with swords and horses'. Newcastle subsequently advised Leven that he could not 'possibly condiscend to any of these propositions.' It did not really matter, for he had succeeded in delaying any concerted attack on the city by a full week.

Hostilities may have been temporarily suspended, but preparations for their renewal with a vengeance had been going on apace. An attempt had already been made to mine Walmgate Bar. Seventeenth century mine laying was a primitive but effective strategy, the aim being to dig a shaft beneath a defensive wall, fill it with gunpowder and then explode the charge. The technology was new to England, having been introduced by Prince Rupert at the Siege of Lichfield in April 1643. On this occasion, however, the perpetrators were discovered and the new Governor, Sir Thomas Glemham, had tunnelled above them, 'powring water in upon them'.

Glemham did not know that there was another tunnel, under St Mary's Tower, by the King's Manor. On 16 June – Trinity Sunday – at noon, the charges beneath St Mary's were exploded, bringing down a portion of it and killing a number of civilians. A Scot, Lieutenant General Crawford, led an assault party of 500 men into the breach and occupied the King's Manor. It seems that Crawford acted precipitately, the original plan being to co-ordinate attacks at various points so as to draw attention away from him. The result was that Crawford and his men were cut off, his command suffering some 300 casualties. Sir Thomas Fairfax remarks that Crawford, 'ambitious to have the honour alone of springing the mine' should have been called to account, 'but that he escaped the better by reason of this triumviral government'. Manchester reported the incident in rather more glowing terms, claiming that the springing of the mine:

> '...did great execution upon the enemy, blowing up a tower which joined to the Manor-yard, and this mine taking so great an effect my Major General commanded 600 men to storm the Manor House, who beat the enemy and took 100 prisoners.'

Much was made of the fact that the attack had been launched on

A Victorian artist's impression of Roundhead troopers attempting to extinguish fires set by the Cavaliers in the houses adjacent to Walmgate Bar.

a Sunday, while everyone was in church. Cavaliers drew attention to the fact that 'in all the whole time of the Siege, there was not any one Person (that I could hear of) did (in the Church) receive the least Harm'. The allies also thought that they had a monopoly on Divine intervention, in support of which a number of miraculous incidents were reported:

'A Cannon bullet was shot through the Tent wherein Generall Lesley, some Scots Commanders and others were, yet no one killed or hurt. A Cannon bullet took off the

31

YORKE

St Mary's Tower was blown up on Trinity Sunday, 16 June, 1644

The Lords place

Mary Gate

Gylly Gate

Roulam

Ouse flu

Fose bridge

Ouse flu

John Speed's map of seventeenth century York. Note the position of the 'King's Fishpond', forming a 'natural' barrier between the Red Tower and Layerthorpe Postern.

Monke bridge

Fos flu

Layrrop Poftern

St Johns Grene

Attempt made to explode a mine under Walmgate Bar

Wan Gate

V

W

A	St Mauri
B	St Peters
C	Belfrey Church
D	S. Maryes Abbey
E	St Martines
F	St Helens
G	Trinite Church
H	St Andrewes
I	St Cuthberts
K	St Saviours
L	Chrifts Church
M	St Sampfons
N	Croufe Church
O	Alhallowes
P	St Michaels
Q	St Maryes
R	St Denis
S	St Margarets
T	St Georges
V	St Laurence
W	St Nicholas
X	Alhallowes
Y	Trinity Abbey
Z	St Iohns
3	St Loyes
4	St Martines
5	St Mary Bifhop E
6	St Mary Bifhop Y
7	Boudam Baxe

8	Peter Gate
9	Collier Gate
10	Goodram Gate
11	Monke Gate
12	Aldwarks
13	St Antonyes Hofpital
14	Coneve ftrete
15	Blake ftrete
16	Stone Gate
17	Oufe Bridge
18	Thurfdayes mark
19	Lepper Gate
20	The Pauement
21	Chfferds Towre
22	The Caftle
23	Fynkle ftret

crowne of a Souldiers hat and the man preserved. Another lying on the ground, the bullet of a Cannon grazeing, took off the heele of his shooe, skratched his foot, and did no more harme.'

A number of civilians had been killed when St Mary's Tower fell. As luck would have it, the Tower had also housed many priceless manuscripts – records of the great religious houses of the north, stored there following the Dissolution of the Monasteries a century before. Both sides, within and without the walls, searched the rubble for surviving documents, Sir Thomas Fairfax offering a reward to any of his men who rescued documents from the ruins.

After the King's Manor fiasco, although a steady artillery barrage was maintained, the Roundheads mounted no further major initiative. Many of the besieging troops had fallen ill and supplies were running short. Lord Fairfax bemoaned the need for 'gunpowder, match and bullet for my own and the Scotch armies in very large proportions', while his army payroll amounted to £4,000 per month, he having received only £10,000 to cover the previous four months. The Cavaliers were also feeling the pinch, Sir Henry Slingsby remarking that 'our provisions still wast'd & would have an end without we had releife'. The noose around the city was now tied so tightly that all contact with the outside world was lost. Newcastle was reduced to communicating with the Cavalier garrison at Pontefract by smoke signals, lighting fires, according to Slingsby, 'upon the top of the Minster', to be answered 'with like signals from Pontefract'.

Hard pressed he may have been, but Newcastle was not beaten. In the early hours of 24 June, a party of Cavaliers about 600 strong attacked the Earl of Manchester's positions. Although repulsed, the assault did nothing to bolster the Roundheads' flagging morale. Such forays were intended to convey the impression that conditions inside the walls were really not so bad. As it happened, the façade would not have to be maintained much longer, for Prince Rupert was, at long last, on his way.

Chapter 3

RUPERT'S RELIEF MARCH

upert had begun the war as commander of the King's cavalry. At Edgehill, the first substantial clash of arms, Rupert commanded the cavalry on the right wing. Although he chased much of the enemy horse from the field, his absence allowed the Roundhead cavalry reserves to mount a successful assault on the Cavalier artillery positions. On this occasion, Rupert returned in time to save the day. Three years later, at Naseby, he would not be so lucky. Following Edgehill, Rupert participated in the capture of Cirencester. He also took Birmingham and Lichfield. On 18 June 1643, he won a skirmish at Chalgrove and three months later, was at the First Battle of Newbury.

Prince Rupert of the Rhine, son of the Elector Palatine, Frederick V, and James I's daughter, Elizabeth. Ripley Castle

As time wore on, Charles grew more and more dependent upon him, for the Prince had one particular advantage over the other Cavalier generals – mobility. At a moment's notice, he could be despatched to any trouble spot in the kingdom. The disadvantage of over-dependency upon a loose cannon lay in the natural resentment of local magnates who, having raised and financed armies for the defence of their 'patch', were expected to gracefully relinquish command when Rupert arrived on the scene.

On 21 March 1644, Rupert succeeded in relieving Newark, where Sir Richard Byron and the Cavalier garrison had been besieged by Sir John Meldrum's Roundhead forces since 29 February. A surprise dawn attack, made before the arrival of the main body of Cavaliers, scattered the besiegers. Rupert himself, 'having advanced so far into the Enemies Ranks, that being observed and known, was dangerously assaulted by three sturdy Souldiers'. Like Sir Thomas Fairfax, he believed in leading from the front, regardless both of his personal safety and his

Newark Castle

On 21 March 1644, Prince Rupert relieved Newark (pictured) and Newcastle hoped that he would proceed into Yorkshire. Instead, he returned to Shrewsbury, leaving York to endure a lengthy siege. (Newark Castle, although a strongpoint, was outdated, its stone walls vulnerable to cannon fire.)

responsibilities as a commander. With Newark secured for the time being, Rupert declined Byron's invitation to stay on, returning instead to his own base at Shrewsbury to immerse himself in the ongoing process of training and recruitment.

On 25 April, with York already under siege, Rupert was called to Oxford, to discuss strategy. The King's major worry was the threat to Oxford posed by the Roundhead armies of Sir William Waller and the Earl of Essex. Rupert recommended reinforcing the garrisons of Banbury, Reading, Wallingford and Abingdon. A strong body of horse should be allocated to the defence of Oxford, while additional cavalry should, he thought, be despatched to reinforce his brother, Prince Maurice, in the West Country. Rupert returned to Shrewsbury on 5 May, finally leaving for York on 16 May at the head of 6,000 infantry and 2,000 horse. His good advice for the defence of central England was, in the end, ignored,

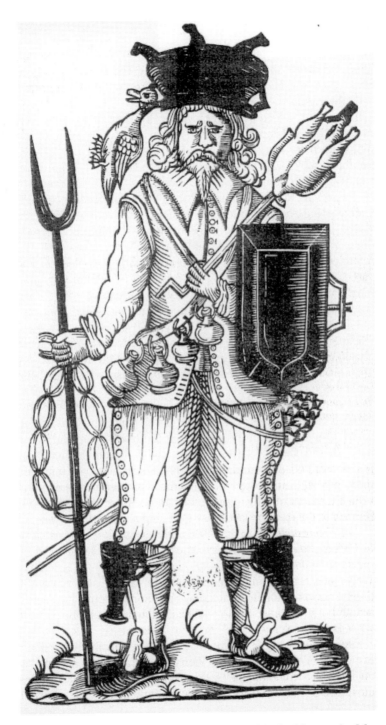

As this satirical sketch suggests, the armies of both sides survived by living off the land. En route to York, Rupert's cavalry mounts created a problem simply by trampling fields in which they were put to graze.

the decision being taken to withdraw into Oxford. Reading and Abingdon were abandoned, thus allowing Essex and Waller to advance on the King's capital far more freely than should have been the case.

The route selected by Rupert for his march to York was anything but direct. On 6 May, he reached Petton, moving on via Whitchurch to Market Drayton. He was at Betley on 21 May, Sandbach on 22 May and at Knustsford the day after. From here, he advanced to Stockport, where his troops 'beat their way over ye Passe'. A Roundhead force of 3,000 men, under colonels Mainwearing and Dukinfield, formed a defensive line before the bridge, while musketeers were deployed behind hedgerows, along which the Cavaliers had to ride. Nevertheless, all the defenders were driven back into the town with heavy losses. The Earl of Manchester, having foreseen this eventuality, had despatched Sir John Meldrum with two regiments of infantry and two troops of horse to bolster Stockport's defences, but Meldrum had arrived too late.

Rupert's success at Stockport had two significant consequences. First it secured a passage over the River Mersey and, second, it led to the relief of Lathom House, which had been under siege since February 1644. Lathom was one of a number of Cavalier-held domiciles ably defended by a woman – in this instance the Countess of Derby. Her husband, the 7th Earl of Derby, was engaged in the defence of the Isle of Man and it had fallen to the Countess to save the family home. Lathom was heavily fortified, surrounded by a moat and with cannon mounted upon each of its nine towers. Sir Thomas Fairfax had attempted to reduce Lathom during one of his forays into Lancashire. Sir Thomas had asked the Countess to consider that Lathom was:

> 'a receptacle of great incurragement to the Papest & inaffected parson in those partes, which I cannot beleeve your Ladyship doth naturally affect.'

The Countess told him to do his worst, being ready to receive the 'utmost violence' of her enemies. Sir Thomas must have been thankful to be recalled into Yorkshire by his father, in the prelude to the Battle of Selby.

The siege was left in the hands of his cousin, Sir William Fairfax and Colonel Alexander Rigby. The Countess responded in similarly vigorous terms to Rigby's summons to surrender, informing him that he was an 'insolent rebel' and that 'he shall

The Earl of Derby was held responsible for depredations committed during Rupert's sack of Bolton and was executed in 1651.

have neither persons, goods nor house.' Her fortitude was rewarded with the arrival of Rupert – fittingly accompanied by Lord Derby – on 25 May, Rigby having fled to Bolton on the Prince's approach.

With an army now 11,000 strong, Rupert went on to storm Bolton. Rigby's troops – 2,000 armed men and 1,500 clubmen – were forced back within their lines and the town overrun. According to Manchester, the Cavaliers 'made a great slaughter of the defenders as the vulgar reports tell us'. Rupert admitted that 'a great slaughter was made of the Enemy', yet Rigby claimed that he lost only around 200 men. If a garrison refused to surrender – and Rigby had been given an opportunity to submit – then it was a case of 'gloves off', with no quarter being given or expected. Therefore, it is likely that atrocities did occur. It suited the Roundhead propaganda machine to exaggerate the degree of depredation, as it suited Cavalier apologists to concentrate on Rupert's extension of mercy to 700 defenders who took refuge in a church. Either way, it was an unfortunate incident which did nothing to further the Cavalier cause in the staunchly Parliamentarian Bolton and district.

From Bolton, Rupert marched to Bury, where he met with Lord Goring's cavalry. At Wigan, he received an enthusiastic welcome – less so at Roundhead Liverpool. He appeared before the town on 7 June. After some initial resistance, the Roundhead governor made good his escape by sea and, on 11 June, the garrison capitulated. A Cavalier garrison was installed and work started on additional fortifications to help ensure the security of what was, for the King, a valuable seaport which facilitated communication with Ireland. It was while he was at Liverpool that Rupert received what turned out to be the most significant letter the King would ever write.

Dated 14 June and written at Ticknall, the letter ran as follows:

'Nepueu/first I must congratulate with you, for your good successes [the taking of Stockport and Bolton], *asseuring you that the things themselfes ar no more welcome to me, than that you are the means: I know the importance of the supplying you with powder for which I have taken all possible wais, having sent both to Ireland & Bristow, as from Oxford this bearer is well satisfied, that it is impossible to have at present, but if he tell you that I may spare them hence, I leave you to judge, having but 36 left; but what I can gett from Bristow (of wch there is not much certaintie, it being threatned to be besieged) you shall have.'*

One wonders whether Rupert was able to ascertain from this intelligence whether he was likely to acquire the supplies he needed. However, the King had clearly started as he meant to continue:

'But now I must give you the true state of my affairs which, if their condition be such as enforces me to give you more peremptory commands than I would willingly do, you must not take it ill. If York be lost, I shall esteem my crown little less, unless supported by your sudden march to me and miraculous conquest in the south, before the effects of the northern power can be found here; but if York be relieved and you beat the rebel armies of both kingdoms which are before it, then but otherwise not, I may possibly make a shift (upon the defensive) *to spin out time until you come to assist me: wherefore I command and conjure you, by the duty and affection which I know you bear me, that (all new enterprises laid aside) you immediately march (according to your first intention) with all your force to the relief of York; but that if that be either lost, or have freed themselves from the besiegers, or that for want of powder you cannot undertake that work; that you immediately march, with your whole strength, to Worcester, to assist me and my army, without which, or your having relieved York by beating the Scots, all the successes you can afterwards have, most infallibly, will be useless unto me: You may believe that nothing but an extreme necessity could make me write thus unto you, wherefore, in this case, I can no ways doubt of your punctual compliance with'*

The letter, signed 'Your loving Uncle and most faithful friend, Charles R', and hardly a model of plain English, is still the subject

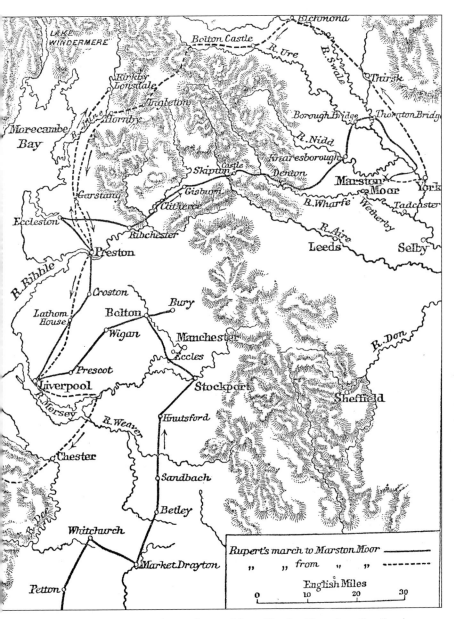

The routes of Prince Rupert's march to and from Marston Moor, from Gardiner's History of the Great Civil War.

of debate. Rupert, ever anxious to perform miracles in order to please the King, thought that Charles was encouraging him to lift the Siege of York, defeat the combined armies of Manchester, Fairfax and Leven in battle and then march south to his uncle's aid. A more cautious commander might have grasped the escape clause – 'if... for want of powder you cannot undertake that work' – and set off for Worcester, but Rupert was not of that ilk. He would set out to achieve everything that might be expected of him.

The letter itself may have been confusing, simply because it represented a cacophony of views. Arguably, according to conspiracy theorists, Lord Digby may have made a significant contribution with a view to either confusing the Prince or forcing him into an impossible situation. Digby and Rupert were implacable enemies. Like the Earl of Clarendon, Digby wielded considerable influence at court while Rupert, continuously in the field, had little time for courtly intrigue, although he did keep in touch with events in Oxford. Occasionally, the news he received succeeded in ruffling his feathers. While at Lathom House, which he had made his headquarters, he received intelligence to the effect that ' the king growes dayly more and more jealous of him and his army', information which, however erroneous it may have been, upsetting to him to such an extent that he delayed his march towards Yorkshire for ten days.

Despite the petty politics and internal bickering, it seems unlikely that Digby, a devout Catholic, would take his dislike of Rupert so far as to embark on a course of action which might result in victory for the Puritans. As far as Charles' letter was concerned, the style probably merely reflected the indecisiveness which was such a fatal flaw in the Stuart character and which would be displayed again a century later by Charles Edward Stuart on the battlefield of Culloden.

Rupert finally moved on, reaching Preston, on 22 June. From there, he marched to Ribchester and Clitheroe, arriving at Gisburn in Yorkshire on 25 June. On the 26 June, he captured and torched Thornton Hall, home of Sir William Lister and a key Roundhead stronghold. Later on the same day, he reached Skipton Castle, home of the Earl of Cumberland and held for the Cavaliers by Sir John Mallory. He remained here for three days, while his men were drilled and messengers were sent on to York.

It may have been in his mind to develop Skipton into a base

which the Roundhead armies investing York might be seduced into attacking. At the very least, it was a secure facility to which, if pressed, he could withdraw. Moving on, he turned south east towards Ilkley. He passed the night of 29 June at Denton, one of the Fairfax estates – birthplace of Sir Thomas – which he occupied. Mindful of the fact that two Fairfaxes, William and John, had died in the defence of the Palatinate, Rupert ensured that the house was not ransacked. The following day, 30 June, he was at Knaresborough Castle, ready to advance on York, just fourteen miles away.

The allies were themselves now in a precarious situation. Reinforcements led by the Earl of Denbigh and Sir John Meldrum would not arrive for several days. They had no choice but to meet the threat posed by Rupert's approach by concentrating their manpower. Thus, they raised the siege and on the evening of 29/30 June, marched out to meet the Prince – even though this meant abandoning valuable stores, including 'mortar pieces, ammunition, war and other carriages, together with four thousand pairs of boots and shoes.' They would block Rupert's road to York and force him to give battle on ground of their own choosing. The site selected was five miles from York, to the west of the village of Long Marston.

In fact, Rupert had no intention of being led to the slaughter so easily. He was determined to reach York and to add Newcastle's garrison to his own strength. On 1 July, he despatched a body of cavalry to Skip Bridge, about a mile to the north west of Long Marston, to encourage the allies in their belief that he would be arriving hotfoot from Knaresborough. They waited in vain, for he had embarked on a forced march of twenty-two miles which would take him north east to Boroughbridge, where he crossed the River Ure. From Boroughbridge, he continued north east, through Milby, after which he could have swung east to effect a crossing of the River Swale at Myton. Instead, he pressed on to Thornton Bridge, then turned south to the Forest of Galtres and the uncontested northern approach to York, via Brafferton, Helperby and Tollerton. He even managed to capture Leven's bridge of boats at Poppleton.

An ecstatic Newcastle sent a note of welcome – the first mistake of the Marston Moor campaign. After extolling him as 'the redemer of the North & the savior of the Crowne', Newcastle assured Rupert that 'I am made of nothing butt thankfulnesse &

obedience to your Highnes comandes'. This gave Rupert the impression that Newcastle was prepared to put his garrison at his disposal and, somewhat insensitively, it seems that he did not take the trouble to enter York personally. Remaining outside, in the Forest of Galtres, he sent in Lord Goring who instructed Newcastle and his men to join Rupert at four o'clock in the morning to give battle to the allies.

Swallowing his resentment, Newcastle had the garrison out on parade at two o'clock, only for an argument over pay to erupt. The parade evaporated, many of the men going off to plunder the abandoned allied siege positions. The blame for the fiasco is generally levelled at Lord Eythin, another of Rupert's many enemies. Eythin had allegedly abandoned Rupert to capture and three years' imprisonment in 1638, when both were fighting in Europe in The Thirty Years War. Such charges, which Eythin felt to be unjust, may have fuelled his resentment of the Prince. However, it is likely that the 'mutiny' occurred spontaneously, without any malice aforethought on the part of Eythin. The garrison was owed several weeks' pay and, after holding out for ten weeks against heavy odds, they found themselves being ordered to turn out in the middle of the night to fight a battle. It would have been unusual, indeed, if there had not been a barrack room lawyer or two on hand to stir up unrest.

When Newcastle failed to put in an appearance, Rupert set out for Marston Moor without him. The allies, for the most part, had passed a poor night out in the open. They had no idea that the Prince intended to fight. His main objective, they presumed, had been the relief of York which, by his brilliant manoeuvre, he had achieved. It was possible that his next move would be to march south to link up with the King's army. The priority, therefore, was to bar his way and, to this end, they decided to proceed via Tadcaster to Cawood and Selby, to defend the crossings of the Rivers Wharfe and Ouse respectively.

On the morning of 2 July, with the Scots leading the way, the allies set off on the first stage of their march. The generals, accompanied by a strong body of horse and dragoons, tarried in the vicinity of Long Marston to cover what amounted to a tactical retreat. They had expected a Cavalier advance guard to appear, and a body of cavalry did arrive on the Moor. It was soon joined by others and it became apparent, to the consternation of Leven, Manchester and Fairfax, that Rupert was in the act of

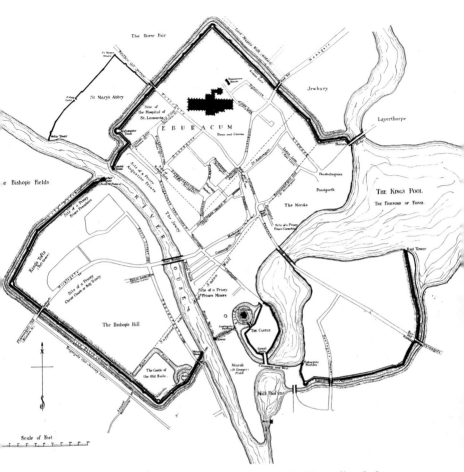

By the time of the Civil War, 'The King's Pool', shown in this medieval plan of York, had shrunk and was in the process of drying up, yet still constituted a significant obstacle to the allies.

bringing up his entire army. The allied infantry, strung out along the Tadcaster road, was extremely vulnerable.

As the triumvirate were making frantic efforts to regroup, Rupert was fretting over Newcastle. Had he not confidently expected the Marquis, he would have attacked the allies while they were on the march. In fact, Newcastle had eventually left York by Micklegate, taking an old track leading to the village of Hessay, to the north east of Long Marston, arriving on Marston Moor, at sometime between nine and eleven o'clock. 'My lord,'

45

said Rupert, 'I wish you had come sooner with your forces, but I hope we shall yet have a glorious day.' Newcastle explained that he was accompanied by only a small mounted column and that the main body of his infantry would be arriving later, as soon as Eythin had rounded them up. Rupert must have been beside himself.

Unable to believe their luck, the allies regrouped, while Rupert remained inactive, awaiting Eythin's arrival with, as Newcastle assured him, 'four thousand as good foot as were in the world.' At some time between two and four o'clock in the afternoon, Eythin finally arrived, bringing with him Newcastle's famous Whitecoats. On their formation in 1642, Newcastle had intended to equip them with scarlet uniforms, but only undyed cloth was available. Later, when the dye became available, they said that they would remain as they were, promising to colour their uniforms with the blood of the enemy. Their coats were, indeed, destined to be coloured with blood, but it was to be their own.

Chapter 4

MARSTON MOOR – PRELUDE

The landscape which greeted Eythin as he joined Rupert and Newcastle was not far removed from that of today. At that time, it was a large tract of open, marshy moor land, covered with gorse or 'whin' bushes. To the north, it was bounded by the River Nidd and Wilstrop Wood, covering a much wider area than it does now. To the west was the village of Tockwith and, running north-south, Sike Beck. To the east was Long Marston and Atterwith Dyke. Joining Syke Beck with Atterwith Dyke was a ditch, bounded by a hedge on its south bank. During the summer months, it would have been quite dry. A number of tracks crossed the moor, creating an intersection about three quarters of a mile up 'Moor Lane'. Eythin would also have noted, to his consternation, that the allies had occupied the area on the south side of the Tockwith/Marston Lanes – ground (under cultivation) which rose to a height of over forty metres. The highest point, opposite Atterwith Lane, was occupied by a clump of trees.

Despite the number of contemporary accounts of the battle, there is still some confusion today over the size of the respective armies. According to Woolrych, the Cavaliers had 'about 18,000 men' and were outnumbered by the allies who were 'nearly half as many again' or 27,000 strong. Rogers states that the cavalry on each side were roughly the same strength, 'probably 7,000', while 'in foot the allies mustered about 20,000 to the Cavaliers' 14,000'. Young's estimate, based on de Gomme, also puts the allied force

Cromwell Plump or Clump Hill from which vantage point the allied generals surveyed the Cavalier positions below.

Sir Thomas Fairfax

Lieutenant-General William Baillie

To Tadcaster

at 27,000, with the Cavaliers at 17,500. Burne gives the total Cavalier strength as 17,000, and that of the allies as 27,000. Newman estimates the total number of participants as 46,000. Leadman states that 'the Puritan hosts ... numbered about 27,000', with the Cavaliers totalling 24,000. Therefore, although the figure of 27,000 for the size of the allied army is generally agreed, there seems to be some confusion over the total strength of the Cavalier army, with estimates varying by up to 10,000 men.

Obviously, it was in the Roundheads' interests to inflate the strength of the Cavalier army. Thus, Sir Thomas Fairfax assessed the enemy strength at 'about 23,000 or 24,000'. Cromwell, writing immediately after the battle, thought it a more modest 20,000. That Prince Rupert had with him something in excess of 14,000 men is likely. The problem revolves around the number of troops which Newcastle had available. According to Edmund Ludlow, a Roundhead officer, Newcastle had with him, in York, 'a garrison consisting of six or seven thousand foot' while, in a letter read to the House of Commons six days after the battle, reference is made to Rupert's army being augmented by 'at least 6000 men out of York'. The latter intelligence may not take account of the fact that Newcastle left three – certainly under strength – regiments to

When Prince Rupert appeared on Marston Moor, the Roundhead army was strung out along the road to Tadcaster. The Scots in the vanguard were only a mile from the town and the bridge spanning the River Wharfe.

guard the city. With a pool of 6,000 men at his disposal, this means that he could not have swelled Rupert's numbers by more than 4,000. Thus, de Gomme's estimate of 17,500 is probably not too wide of the mark, putting the total number of combatants at 44,500 and making Marston Moor the largest battle of the Civil War.

Heavily outnumbered, Rupert must have been only too well aware that a surprise attack, catching the enemy off guard, had been his best chance of victory and that it had now ebbed away. Therefore, he was able to take time out to explain to Newcastle and Eythin what he intended to do. He produced a paper, 'which he said was the draft of the battle as he meant to fight it' and asked them what they thought of it. Eythin replied testily that it looked fine on paper but that 'there is no such thing in the field.' The details of Rupert's plan are not known. There may not have been much detail, but Eythin's criticism was based primarily upon his belief that the Cavalier army was drawn up too closely to the allied lines and on unfavourable ground.

There are many surviving accounts of the battle – although most are, at best, sketchy – but no one seems to have bothered to draw up a detailed plan of the deployment of both armies. The earliest extant attempt to do so was made by Sir Bernard de Gomme nearly

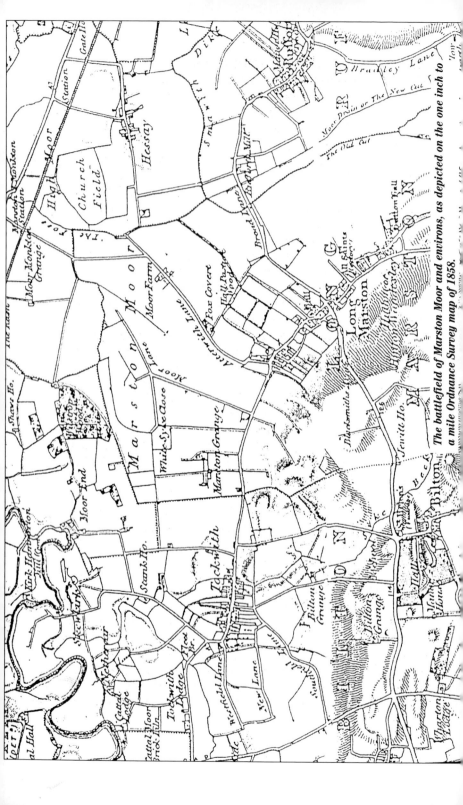

The battlefield of Marston Moor and environs, as depicted on the one inch to a mile Ordnance Survey map of 1858.

twenty years after the event. A Dutch engineer in the employ of the King, de Gomme had designed the defences of Oxford. His plan is thin on detail as far as the allied deployment is concerned. As might be expected, there is far more detail in respect of the Cavaliers although, as Newman has pointed out, some key units go unmentioned, suggesting the omission of late arrivals on the battlefield. Fortunately, in the twentieth century, there came to light a plan of the allied positions, drawn up by Sir James Lumsden, who commanded an infantry regiment on the allied left wing. Therefore, by comparing Lumsden and de Gomme, it is possible to construct a reasonably accurate battle plan.

Not surprisingly, no two plans of the battle as presented by 'modern' writers are identical. For example, Burne (1951) presents three Cavalier groupings: the cavalry of Rupert on the right and Goring on the left, with infantry under Newcastle in the centre, while Woolrych (1961) denotes two lines of Rupert's Horse on the right, two lines of Goring's Horse on the left and infantry in the centre under Eythin. The suggested deployment given below is by no means definitive, the objective being to provide sufficient detail while not allowing preoccupation with the trees to obscure the view of the forest.

For the allies, occupying pride of place on the right wing between Moor Lane and Atterwith Lane was Sir Thomas Fairfax, commanding 4,000 cavalry, some 500 dragoons and 500 musketeers, drawn up in three lines. Sir Thomas led the front line, with Colonel John Lambert leading the second and the Earl of Eglinton the third.

The allied left wing comprised some 4,500 cavalry and dragoons and 600 musketeers. Commanded by Lieutenant-General Oliver Cromwell, it also comprised three lines. Cromwell himself led the first, Colonel Bartholomew Vermuyden probably led the second and Major-General David Leslie led the third.

The spread of infantry units in the centre is more problematical. Gardiner places Lord Fairfax to the right, adjacent to his son, 'Manchester's Army' to the left, by Cromwell, and 'Leven's Army' in the middle. Although this sounds reasonable, it is not borne out by eyewitness accounts, which suggest much more of a mix compatible with the hasty deployment of troops returning from the Tadcaster march. It is probable that to the right of the front line were two brigades of Scots led by Lieutenant-General Baillie – with the Earl of Lindsay and the Earl of Lauderdale on the extreme right. Next to Ballie, in the centre, was a brigade of Lord Fairfax's infantry, with two brigades of Manchester's infantry under Sergeant-Major-General Lawrence Crawford. A second line consisted of Scots under Lumsden, while a third line was made up of another of Manchester's brigades on the right, a Scots brigade in the centre and two more of Fairfax's brigades on the left. Leven, in overall command, may have remained on high ground to the rear, with his artillery and another Scots brigade.

On the Cavalier right wing, facing Cromwell, was a front line of about 1,100 horse and 800 musketeers in the overall command of Lord Byron and made up of Byron's own regiment, together with regiments led by Colonel Marcus Trevor, Sir William Vaughan and Sir John Urry. A second line comprised 800 horse under Lord Molyneux and included the regiments of Sir Thomas Tyldesley and Prince Rupert. On the extreme right was Colonel Samuel Tuke's regiment.

Marston Hall depicted in the late nineteenth century.

On the left wing, opposing Sir Thomas Fairfax, was Lord Goring, with 1,100 cavalry and 500 musketeers, the latter being placed in units of 50 between the regiments of horse, the front line of which included units commanded by Colonel Carnaby on the far left, Sir Charles Lucas, Sir Marmaduke Langdale, Colonel Eyre and Colonel Frescheville.

The infantry in the centre comprised a front line of regiments under Major-General Henry Tillier and included Sir Thomas Tyldesley's infantry regiment and those of Colonels Warren, Erneley and Gibson. A second line, including the regiments of Colonels Chisenall, Cheater and Milward may have been commanded by Eythin and Sir Francis Mackworth.

To the rear of the second infantry line was Sir William Blakeston's brigade of horse and, behind Blakeston, more divisions of Newcastle's infantry, some of which – including the Whitecoats – were still arriving when battle commenced. In the extreme rear were Lord Widdrington's brigade of horse, Prince Rupert's Lifeguard and the Prince himself. Often placed alongside Rupert is Commissary-General George Porter's troop of horse. Porter had fought with Rupert at the relief of Newark and Rupert thought him incompetent. The place where he could do least damage would be where the Prince could keep a close eye on him.

De Gomme makes no mention of who was in overall command of the Cavalier infantry. It should have been Newcastle, but it wasn't. It could have been Eythin, with Tillier and Sir Francis Mackworth serving as his subordinate commanders, the confusion here perhaps reflecting the Cavaliers' unpreparedness for battle – although they had gone so far as to line a length of the ditch with musketeers under Colonel Thomas Napier, commanding a 'Forlorn Hope', together with some light artillery.

The armies were only half a mile apart, the allied line occupying the ridge of high ground to the south of Marston and Tockwith Lanes, with the Cavaliers deployed behind the ditch to the north. Eythin appears to have voiced concern at the close proximity of the enemy and at the advantage conferred by their position, but Rupert was sure that it was now too late in the day – towards seven o'clock – for any fighting to take place. The following morning would be soon enough, when he himself would take the initiative by launching an attack. Concurring, for he had little choice but to do otherwise, Newcastle retired to his carriage to smoke 'a pype of tobacco'.

The enemies of the Marquis were ready to remark upon his apparent indolence. In his defence, he may have quitted the field at the suggestion of Rupert. Newcastle, too, had been fretting at the prospect of an allied assault, and the Prince, who seems to have regarded him as someone to be humoured, like an influential elderly relative suffering from senile dementia, was anxious to put him to bed. The very fact that Newcastle had a coach at all has been criticised. Rupert, after all, was soon 'set upon the earth at meat.' However, Newcastle's coach was his mobile headquarters, and with him he had to carry all the paraphernalia, including papers and despatches, necessary to the management of an army on the move.

William Cavendish, Earl of Newcastle, was created a Marquis in Octovber 1443 for his successes in the North.

Rupert did not dine with his men, but set himself apart, 'a pretty distance from his troops'. The army had little in the way of food and, such was his degree of confidence that the allies would not attack, that he gave orders for provisions to be brought from York although, considering the exigencies of the siege, it is to be doubted whether there was much in the way of sustenance to be had. Each man made himself as comfortable as the circumstances permitted. Newcastle, admittedly more comfortable than anyone else, had barely lit his pipe when he heard 'a great noise and thunder of shooting'. Rupert had got it wrong.

Chapter 5

MARSTON MOOR I

T he Earl of Leven may have permitted Rupert to select the place of battle, but he had no intention of allowing him to choose the time. The late arrival of Eythin and the infantry from York provided him with a golden opportunity to catch the enemy off guard. While the new arrivals were being accommodated in the centre and with everyone else apparently in the act of settling down for the night, Leven ordered a general advance.

The Civil War witnessed much skulduggery and duplicity but, where a major set-piece battle was concerned, it was still unacceptable to assault chaps before they were ready. The

Gardiner's plan of Marston Moor (c.1888).

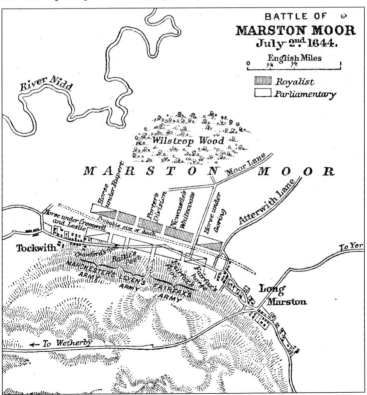

proliferation of weak excuses that were put forward by the allies suggests that they were acutely aware of the situation. Scoutmaster-General Watson argues:

> '...surely had two such Armies (drawn up so close one to the other, being of both wings within Musket shot), departed without fighting, I think it would have been as great a wonder, as hath been seen in England.'

Thomas Stockdale states that the allies took the initiative because 'the enemy would not advance.' The official dispatch of 'the three generals' ignores the issue all together, averring that 'Before both armies were in readiness it was near seven o'clock at night, about which time they advanced the one toward the other.'

Of course, only the allied army was 'ready' and it was they who advanced. The Cavaliers' first move was made by Byron. As Gardiner points out, Byron may already have been involved in a preliminary skirmish earlier in the day, in which a party of the

Prince Rupert at Marston Moor just prior to the battle.

Lord Byron's cavalry was deployed on either side of Kendal Lane. The lane itself and the hedges on either side are late eighteenth century additions to the landscape.

Cavalier horse had tried unsuccessfully to 'win ground on the extreme left of the Parliamentary ground at Tockwith.' Since then, he had been under instructions to stay put, being situated 'behind a warren and a slough'. The nature of the ground, coupled with the supporting firepower of the musketeers at his disposal would, Rupert felt, ensure that any attack would prove 'dangerous if not ruinous' to the allies. In his character, Byron – an ancestor of the poet – was not unlike his general in terms of impetuosity, although it was thought by some that he had been urged on by Colonel Urry.

The role played by Urry in the Battle of Marston Moor is unclear. A notorious turncoat, Urry had started out as a Roundhead, serving with the Earl of Essex. Early in 1643, he had attached himself to Rupert, resuming his allegiance to Parliament after Marston Moor, informing Sir William Waller's Roundhead army of the Cavaliers' strength prior to the Second Battle of Newbury. In 1645, he fought for the Covenanters against the Marquess of Montrose's Royalist army, and after the Battle of Auldern transferred his allegiance to Montrose, with whom he was hanged in 1650. Sir Hugh Cholmeley, himself a turncoat, stated that at Marston Moor:

> 'a Scottish officer among the Prince... fled to the Parliament army and gave them intelligence; and it was further observed that Urry, a Scotchman, having the marshalling of the horse on the Prince's right wing, his own troop were the first that turned their backs...'

Perhaps Cholmeley's suspicions were influenced by Urry's subsequent actions before Newbury, but they cannot wholly be dismissed.

In Byron's favour, it can be said that it had begun to rain and Napier's musketeers were probably experiencing some difficulty in lighting their matches. In any event, there was no advantage to be gained by providing the Roundhead gunners – who were far too close for comfort – with sitting targets.

Cromwell, who had been contemplating the problem of assaulting Byron's position, must have been relieved when he observed the Cavalier advance. According to Slingsby, Cromwell:

> 'came off the Cony Warren, by Bilton Bream, to charge our horse, and upon their first charge routed them; they fly along by Wilstrop woodside as fast and as thick could be.'

The Cavaliers did retreat by Wilstrop Wood, but not before

THE SOULDIERS

Pocket Bible :

Containing the moſt (if not all) thoſe places contained in holy Scripture, which doe ſhew the qualifications of his inner man, that is a fir Souldier to fight the Lords Battels, both before he ſight, in the fight, and after the fight ;

Which Scriptures are reduced to ſeverall heads, and ſitly applyed to the Souldiers ſeverall occaſions, and ſo may ſupply the want of the whole Bible; which a Souldier cannot conveniently carry about him :

And may bee alſo uſefull for any Chriſtian to meditate upon, now in this miſerable time of Warre.

Imprimatur, *Edm. Calamy:*

*Joſ.*18. This Book of the Law ſhall not depart out of thy mouth, but thou ſhalt meditate therein day and night, that thou maiſt obſerve to doe according to all that is written therein, for then thou ſhalt make thy way proſperous, and have good ſucceſſe.

Printed at *London* by *G.B.* and *R.W.* for *G.C.* 1643.
*Aug:*3ᵈ

Perhaps religious fanaticism played a part in the allied victory at Marston Moor. Doubtless, there was much singing of psalms in the ranks before the battle, while some troopers may have carried copies of 'The Souldiers Pocket Bible'.

putting up a stout resistance. While Byron's front line broke, his second line held firm standing, as Lord Saye remarks, 'like an Iron Wall'. For a while, therefore, the outcome was in some doubt.

Also in some doubt was Cromwell's role, because after breaking through Byron's front line, he was wounded and probably had to retire from the field. It was a minor wound in the neck and there are conflicting stories as to how it was sustained. One story involves his being shot accidentally by one of his own men. The Cavalier, Colonel Trevor, also claimed responsibility, alleging that he wounded Cromwell with his sword. Critics would later claim that he had withdrawn in order to avoid the worst of the fighting, Crawford asserting that Cromwell's wound was but 'a little burn in the neck'. Other accounts refer specifically to a pistol fired at close range, causing powder burns and a temporary loss of vision. Whatever the extent of the wound, it is believed that

It is thought that artillery – as depicted here by a Victorian artist – played a minor role in the battle. There was an exchange of artillery fire early in the day, but the allied attack, when it came, depended for its success upon the element of surprise.

Battlefield ➡

Sike Beck, in the village of Tockwith, marking the extreme western edge of the battlefield.

Cromwell was helped to a cottage in Tockwith, where he had it dressed.

We do not know how long he was away, but fierce hand-to-hand fighting continued in his absence. Command may have been assumed by David Leslie who must have exercised some skill in holding everything together. Also prominent in this capacity, according to his own account, was Crawford who rallied Cromwell's wavering cavalry by reviling them as 'poltroons and cowards'. The important point is that the two front lines did hold firm and that this was due as much to their training as to any qualities of leadership which Leslie and/or Crawford may have brought to the situation.

As Byron advanced, Napier's contribution came to a premature end. With Byron's cavalry, inter-mingled with enemy horse, before them, the musketeers had lost their capacity for subjecting the enemy to concentrated volleys of fire as they themselves became targets of the allied cavalry. Forgetting his role as commander-in-chief, Rupert galloped off to place himself as the head of his own faltering Lifeguard. Sir Hugh Cholmley states that Rupert encountered his men 'turning their backs to the enemy'. He managed to rally them 'but fruitlessly, the enemy having before broken the force of that wing, and without any great difficulty, for these troops which formerly had been thought unconquerable, now upon a panic fear...took scare and most fled.'

A significant contributory reason for the allied success on this wing was that Byron was heavily outnumbered. The mettle of Crawford's infantry, too, is worthy of mention, Lumsden referring to their 'good service'. Lumsden also praises Cromwell and Leslie who 'carried themselves bravely

Major-General David Leslie, whose support of Cromwell proved vital to the Roundhead victory.

and under God was one main occasion for our victory.' Cromwell himself was less generous, dismissing Leslie and his men rather sourly as 'a few Scots in our rear'.

Cromwell had very firm ideas as far as the raising and training of men was concerned. With regard to the selection of 'captains of horse', he thought 'a few honest men are better than numbers' and that he would 'rather have a plain russet-coated captain that knows what he fights for, and loves what he knows than that which you call a gentleman and is nothing else.' He wanted 'honest, sober Christians' who expected 'to be used as men.' One critic referred to Cromwell's troops as 'a swarm... of those that call themselves the godly', some of whom had even 'seen visions and had revelations.' Bigots and fanatics they may have been, but they displayed a commitment of a kind unknown to the 'old decayed servingmen and tapsters' who had enlisted with the Earl of Essex to fight at Edgehill.

The commitment of the Cavaliers themselves is not in doubt. Their cavalry 'being many of them, if not the greatest part Gentlemen, stood very firm', but the courage they displayed as individuals would not have equalled the group discipline and solidarity of Cromwell's 'Ironsides' – a term supposedly coined by Rupert after the battle. As far as the quality of mounts is concerned, those of Cavalier and Roundhead were probably evenly matched, although it is tempting to think of the Ironsides' mounts as a shade stronger and heavier. The Scots' horses were traditionally smaller and lighter, Lord Saye dismissing them as 'weak nags' and yet, without Leslie's support, Cromwell may not have carried the day on his wing. Significantly, at Naseby, he would place himself at the head of his second line, putting into practice the two lessons he had

Oliver Cromwell

learned at Marston Moor: the perils of overexposing himself to personal danger and the importance of ensuring that he had a dependable rear line to support the first.

On this occasion, Cromwell, back in the saddle, seemed to be carrying all before him. Most contemporary accounts suggest that Cromwell's accomplishment in sweeping aside Byron was quite straight forward – little more than a formality. Sir Thomas Fairfax, however, described the fighting here as being 'performed for a while with much resolution on both sides' and one would probably describe Cromwell's progress as steady as opposed to meteoric, with Byron's second line, under Molyneux, offering the stoutest opposition. But progress he did, Crawford's infantry following in his wake, gradually wheeling in upon the enemy infantry's right flank. With the cream of the Cavalier horse broken, surely there was nothing to stand between the Roundheads and total victory?

Chapter 6

MARSTON MOOR II

If all was going well for the allies on their left wing, the situation on the right was developing very differently. Here, Sir Thomas Fairfax was having a far tougher time of it against Lord Goring. Often castigated as a drunkard, Goring was a courageous and astute leader of cavalry, and he had trounced Sir Thomas at Seacroft Moor the previous year, an event which must been to the fore in the minds of both men.

As the whole allied front advanced, Sir Thomas made slow progress, blaming the terrain which was, indeed, difficult. As he moved forward with a vanguard of 400 horse, his progress was impeded by 'whins and ditches which we were to pass over before we could get to the Enemy'. According to Captain Stewart, between Fairfax's cavalry and Goring:

> 'there was no passage but a narrow lane, where they could
> not march above 3 or 4 in front, upon the one side of the

The Royalist and Parliamentarian positions according to the battlefield plan situated to the rear of the monument.

Lane was a Ditch, and on the other a Hedge, both whereof were lined with musketeers.'

When Fairfax charged, the enemy kept formation, 'receiving them by threes and fours as they marched out of the Lane.' Clearly, unlike Byron, Goring was quite content to stand his ground, allowing Fairfax to negotiate all obstacles. For good measure, the Cavalier musketeers kept up a heavy fire which, said Fairfax, 'did us much hurt.'

When Sir Thomas did break through, there was a lengthy tussle, during which the ground was 'hotly disputed... at sword point.' Sir Thomas was slashed across the face by a sabre and his horse almost felled by a musket ball. His men pushed on through the Cavalier lines, perhaps with the sole aim of reaching open ground. There was even a suggestion that they were purposely let through. As for Sir Thomas himself, he wheeled around – yet again in the middle of a battle – to find himself alone, 'in among the Enemy, which stood up and down the Field in several bodies of Horse.' Removing the white favour which distinguished him as one of the enemy, from his hat, he 'passed through for one of their [the Cavaliers'] own Commanders', making his way over to the allied left wing. It was an exploit worthy of 'The Rider of the White Horse', but far more in keeping with Sir Thomas's earlier guerrilla campaigns than with his responsibilities as a senior commander in a major set-piece battle. As Sir James Lumsden remarked, despite Fairfax's personal bravery, 'his horse answered not our expectation, nor his worth.'

Sir Thomas's failure to rein in the men who had charged with him meant that they left the field, some in quest of safety, others in pursuit of some of the enemy horse which they had swept before them. In his accounts of the battles in which he was engaged, Fairfax, like Cromwell, generally presented himself in the best possible light. With regard to this occasion, he later wrote:

> *'We were a long time engaged with one another; but at last we routed that part of their Wing. We charged and pursued them a good way towards York.'*

Fairfax remained very touchy on the subject for the rest of his life. In 1662, Thomas Fuller included a chapter on Yorkshire battles in a book entitled *Worthies of England*. His section on Marston Moor included the statement: 'Goring so valiantly charged the Right Wing of the Enemy, that they fairly forsook the Field.' Fairfax

Sir Thomas Fairfax, 'The Rider of the White Horse' was also known as 'Black Tom' to his friends, because of his swarthy complexion, to the disinterested because of his periodic fits of depression, and to his enemies because of his evil deeds.

went so far as to scribble a note of rebuttal in his own copy. 'I envy none the honour they deservedly got in this battle,' he begins, rather lamely,

'nor am I ambitiously desirous of a branch of their laurel. But I see no reason to be exluded the Lists: in which I underwent equal hazards with any others that day. But being my lot to be cast upon many disadvantages, having command

Cavalier and Roundhead cavalry fight it out at Marston Moor. This illustration dating from the turn of the last century depicts the confusion and chaos at the heart of a Civil War pitched battle.

of the Right Wing, with much difficulty I could get but 5 Troops in order... But, indeed, the rest of the Horse, I could not draw up to charge with me, were soon routed with that part of the Enemy we left behind. But to show that some did their parts: having routed some of the Enemy... few of us came off without dangerous wounds... Which shows that the Right Wing did not wholly leave the Field...'

Scoutmaster-General Watson had another story to tell, based on his observation of Goring's cavalry running riot, 'routing all our Horse and Foot, so that there was not a man left standing before

Goring

Looking East from Moor Lane, marginally to the south of Goring's position – ground over which Sir Thomas Fairfax advanced to engage the Cavalier left wing.

them.' Stewart also states:

> *'Fairfax his new levied regiment being in the van, they wheeled about and being hotly pursued by the enemy, came back upon the Lord Fairfax Foot, and the reserve of the Scottish foot, broke them wholly and trod the most part of them underfoot.'*

At least Stewart notes that Sir Thomas's regiment was 'new levied'. He did have his own Yorkshire regiments, but he also commanded some untried Lancashire regiments in addition to Eglinton's Scots. Fairfax probably decided to keep his Yorkshire men in reserve and to use the Lancashire regiments as cannon fodder. With the benefit of hindsight, one might argue, from the comfort of one's armchair, that he would have been better advised to select his veterans, who would have regrouped and remained on the field.

With the failure of Fairfax's charge, Goring could seize the opportunity to launch a counter-attack. Leaving a reserve under the command of Sir Charles Lucas in possession of his portion of the field, he led a charge up the hill. Initially, Eglinton's Scots offered some resistance, but were eventually turned and fled. Stockdale states that Goring's men:

> *'possess themselves first of our Ordnance, and shortly after our carriages also which they first plundered... and some of the enemy's horse pursued our horse nearly two miles from the field, so that in all appearance the day was lost.'*

Appearances, however, were never more deceptive than on this occasion.

Everything seemed to be going according to plan as Lucas turned his attention to the newly exposed right flank of the allied infantry. From the vantage point previously occupied by the allied command, Goring made what he could of the confusion below him. After his own triumph, he must have been dismayed to see what was

Alexander Leslie, Earl of Leven, leader of the Scottish army which gave the Roundheads the upper hand in the North of England.

happening on the Cavaliers' right wing. He needed to regroup – and quickly – for Cromwell was pushing through to the rear of the enemy lines and, supported by Crawford, was in the act of sweeping eastward. Goring's men, however, had dispersed – unlike Cromwell's troops who had remained on the field, intact, ready to engage in another manoeuvre.

At some juncture, Cromwell was joined by Sir Thomas Fairfax who appraised him of what had occurred on his wing. Did he tell Cromwell the whole story, or just enough to make him understand that, apart from the few troops of Horse which he had managed to round up and which now accompanied him, virtually none of the horse which had started under his command remained on the field? And did Cromwell experience a glow of inward satisfaction in the knowledge that, for the duration of the battle at least, he himself was now leading the Roundhead cavalry?

Desperately, Goring tried to rally as many of his men as possible – perhaps 1,000 or so. He now found himself in a similar position from which Fairfax had started, with the same hostile ground to cross in order to reach Cromwell, as the latter wheeled around towards Atterwith Lane. He might have waited for Cromwell to come to him, but what if Cromwell refused? At best, Goring would be left stranded, able only to stand and watch while Eythin's infantry was surrounded and destroyed. In reality, he had no option but to take the initiative with a view to saving the day. Sir Hugh Cholmeley was of the opinion that if Goring had managed to keep his cavalry intact in the first place, then the battle might have ended in a draw. Even now, as he advanced down the hill, Goring must have hoped that it was not too late to salvage something from the day. Watson referred to the meeting between Goring and Cromwell as 'the business of the day', and while a Cavalier victory was, by this time, unlikely, it was still open to question whether the result would be classed as a defeat or a rout.

Goring was heavily outnumbered and many of his men, like those of Fairfax before him, must have been picked off by musket fire before they reached the Moor. However, those who did break through fought bravely, as is borne out by the casualty lists. Gradually, they were overcome, the encounter breaking up into a series of unco-ordinated fights until the survivors, including Goring, were chased from the field. At least they were well placed to make their escape to York, probably making their way up Atterwith Lane and through Hessay – the road taken by Newcastle on his outward march.

Chapter 7

MARSTON MOOR III

hile heroics were taking place on either wing, the infantry in the middle slogged it out, their fate nonetheless dependent upon the outcome of the cavalry engagements. Crawford, as we have already seen, moved up with Cromwell. To Crawford's right, Lord Fairfax's Foot also pushed forward with some success before being driven back, while Baillie's Scots to the centre right were held by Tillier and Frescheville. Blakeston, seeking to capitalise on the reverse suffered by Fairfax's Foot, bore down on them. At the same time, the cavalry of Sir Charles Lucas attacked the infantry of Lindsay and Lauderdale. Reinforced by Baillie and Lumsden who, perceiving 'the greatest weight of the battle to lie sore upon the Earl of Lindsay's and Lord Maitland's (Lauderdale's) regiment, sent up a reserve'. The latter proved impossible to break and Lucas, unhorsed, was taken prisoner.

As both sides became deprived of cavalry cover on their flanks, the situation in the centre grew unnerving. Byron's collapse and Goring's over-enthusiasm on the Cavalier side, together with the charges of Cromwell and Fairfax for the allies had left the infantry to fend for themselves. Crawford's foot, working closely with

Marston Grange is a rough marker for the centre of the Cavalier line and Tillier's infantry.

Marston Grange

Cavalier Infantry

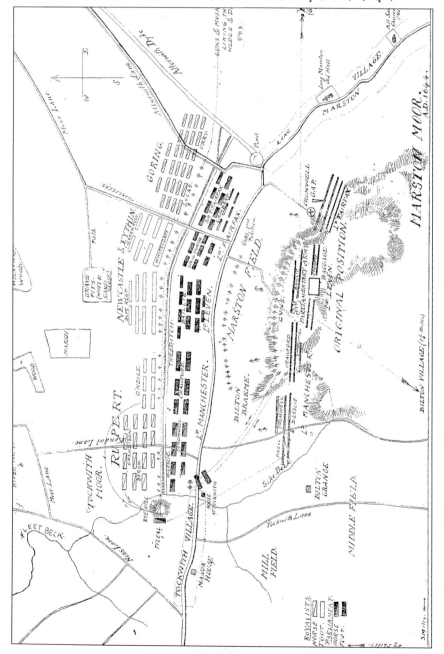

CR B Barrett's plan of Marston Moor (c.1896). According to Barrett, Colonel Urry was on the extreme left of the Cavalier front line, while the house in Tockwith where Cromwell allegedly had his wound dressed is shown on the south side of Tockwith Lane. Although the idea that the ditch did not stretch the whole width of the battlefield, is supposedly a relatively new one, Barrett was aware of the possibility, for he omits a length, remarking that 'the evidence on examination seems to prove that some portion had been filled in eastward of Kendall (sic) Lane.'

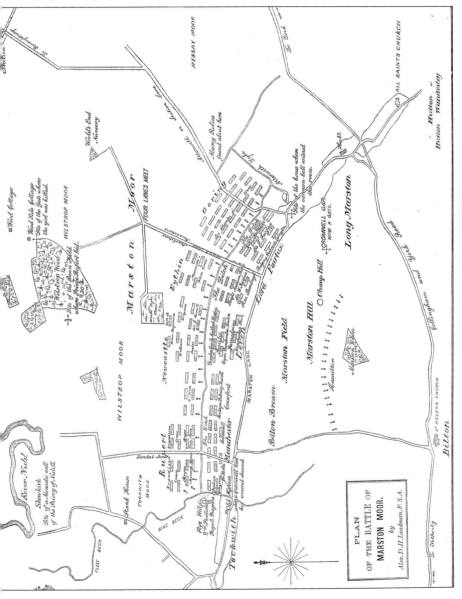

A D H Leadman's plan of Marston Moor (c1891). Like Barret, Leadman puts Colonel Urry on the Cavalier left wing, but shows the ditch running the whole way from Atterwith Dyke to Sike Beck.

PLAN
OF THE BATTLE OF
MARSTON MOOR.
by
Alex.D.H.Leadman, F.S.A.

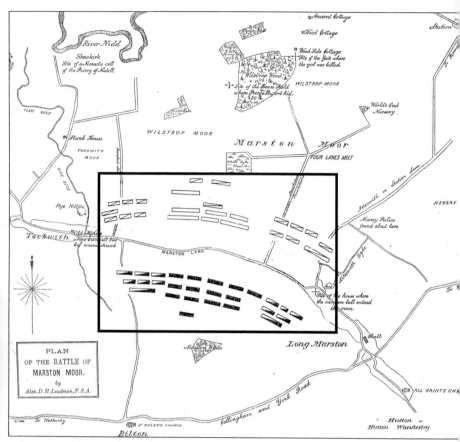

PLAN
OF THE BATTLE OF
MARSTON MOOR.
by
Alex. D. H. Leadman, F.S.A.

Present day interpretation. and below, key to the preliminary Roundhead and Cavalier positions, superimposed on Leadman's plan.

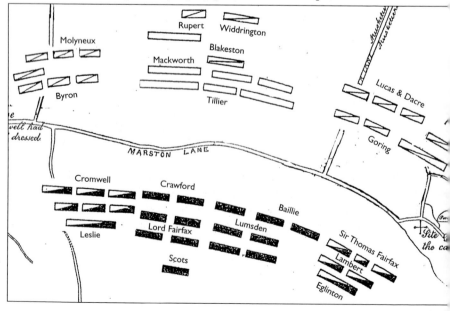

Cromwell, had been able to turn the extreme right Cavalier infantry flank while, ultimately, Cromwell's manoeuvre, to the rear of the Cavalier lines, would threaten the left.

Crawford may have 'overwinged the enemy', but the allies own right flank under Baillie held firm, refusing to be cowed by Goring. Tillier, however, met with more success against Lord Fairfax's Foot in the centre, his efforts being supported by Blakeston's cavalry. Seeing Fairfax's Foot falling back, Blakeston decided to attack and succeeded in scattering them, together with many of Lumsden's Scottish reserves.

Blakeston has been criticised for not having any specific objectives because when he had reached the high ground of Marston Field, having charged through the allied ranks, he lingered, unsure of what to do next. Yet, such inactivity illustrates not a lack of ability on the part of any individual, but the absence of unity in Rupert's army as a whole. There was Napier and his musketeers, Widdrington's Brigade, Newcastle's Whitecoats, the Prince's own Lifeguard, and so on – a veritable pot-pourri, incapable, without firm direction, of participating in any kind of co-ordinated activity. The allied ranks comprised three distinct armies, and the Scots may have been a little untidy, but Fairfax's Yorkshire veterans and the Army of the Eastern Association were established homogeneous forces, each accustomed to fighting in unison.

The disorganisation in the Cavalier ranks is further illustrated by the role played in the battle by Newcastle. His wife states that he:

'...was no sooner got on horseback but he beheld a dismal sight of the horse of His Majesty's right wing, which out of a panic fear had left the field, and run away with all the speed they could.'

Despite the Duchess's best efforts to convey the impression that by the time Newcastle entered the fray, all was lost, it is probable that he spent some little time in trying to locate his Whitecoats and, perhaps, Rupert. He seems to have fallen in with a troop of gentlemen volunteers under Sir Thomas Metham and that they all joined in Blakeston's charge. Newcastle, the Duchess adds, despatched three of the enemy.

While Blakeston tarried on the ridge, he was marked down by the ranks of Manchester's Foot, nearby. Wheeling about, the infantry advanced on Blakeston, forcing him back onto the moor and into conflict with some of the Eastern Association cavalry,

Moor Lane – one of a number of tracks which criss-crossed Marston Moor at the time of the battle – looking north towards 'Four Lanes Meet'.

The use of artillery and muskets at the Battle of Marston Moor should not be allowed to mask the importance of the pike – up to sixteen feet (4.9 metres) in length. Lindsay and Lauderdale 'having interlined their musketeers with pikemen, they made the enemies horse... give ground'.

which proved fatal, many of Blakeston's men being killed or captured. Despite the pugnacity of Manchester's Infantry, however, the allied Foot had been badly shaken by the assaults of Blakeston and Lucas and, of course, that of Goring. Fairfax's Foot fled, together with many of the Scots in the allied centre, crying out 'wae's us, we are all undone.' Lumsden referred to the sorry state of affairs:

'These that showed themselves most basely... they carried not themselves as I would have wished, neither could I prevail with them. For these that fled never came to charge with the enemies, but were so possessed with one panic fear that they

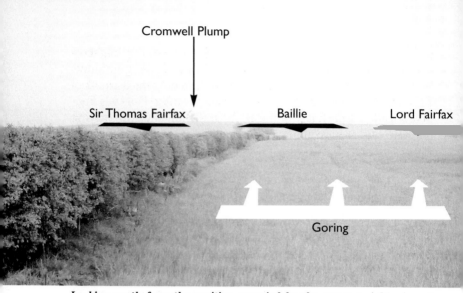

Looking south from the position occupied by the extreme right wing of Goring's cavalry towards 'Cromwell Plump' and the preliminary Allied positions.

> *ran for example to others and no enemy following, which gave the enemy occasion to charge them...'*

At this juncture, the prognosis must have been bleak, for the nerve of all the Allied generals gave way. Leven, Manchester and Fairfax all fled, although the confused stories of how far they ran and what happened when each reached his destination were probably embellished by the enemy. Leven rode all the way to Leeds – twenty miles – where he was arrested by the parish constable. Fairfax rode to his house at Cawood and went to bed. Manchester left the field for a time, and despite some claims that he did not get back until 11.00 pm, an hour after the result came in, it seems more likely that he rallied some of his men and returned much earlier.

Seen in the context of this collapse, the action of Lauderdale and Lindsay in holding Lucas assumes a pivotal role in the Allied victory. The episode also proves that disciplined infantry was well able to hold its own against cavalry, the musketeers and pikemen, making

> *'the enemy's Horse, notwithstanding for all the assistance they had of their foot, at two several assaults to give ground: and in this hot dispute with both they continued for an hour, still maintaining their ground.'*

By this time, the Cavalier Foot was virtually surrounded. Having disposed of the remains of Goring's cavalry, Cromwell could now confine his attention to the enemy infantry. Slingsby says 'although a great while they maintained the fight, yet at last they were cut down and most part either taken or killed.'

Unusually, a portion of the infantry was destined to win some of the glory generally reserved for the cavalry units. As Cromwell made his way towards the position lately occupied by Goring, he came under fire from Hatterwith enclosure, and Newcastle's Whitecoats, trying to give Goring time to regroup. Until then, they had taken no part in the battle. Cromwell could not afford to delay his advance and so he deployed a regiment of Scottish dragoons to tackle them. Valiantly, the Whitecoats kept the dragoons at bay for an hour. It was a matter of honour with them, for they carried Newcastle's regimental colours. Despite being offered quarter, they carried on 'until there was not thirty of them living', each men falling 'in the same order and rank wherein he had fought.' According to an eye-witness account:

'This sole regiment, after the day was lost, having got into a small parcel of ground ditched in, and not of easy access of horse, would take no quarter, and by mere valour for one whole hour kept the troops of horse from entering amongst them at near push of pike... though they could not ride for their wounds, yet were so desperate as to get either a pike or a sword... and to gore the trooper's horses as they came near.'

The battle between Cromwell and Byron was fought out on this ground, to the west of the present-day 'New Row'.

New Row

Cromwell

As far as the battle is concerned, the key phrase here is 'after the day was lost', for the Whitecoats were completely cut off from the main action, their gallant resistance having no effect upon the final outcome. However, there were almost certainly other isolated groups of Cavaliers in the field, reflecting the piecemeal nature of Rupert's army. For example, it is recorded that after taking care of the Whitecoats, Leslie addressed himself to a brigade of 'Greencoats' and that he 'cut off a great number, and put the rest to flight.'

In addition, Sir Philip Monckton, who fought with Goring, claimed that he also remained on the battlefield in command of a body of horse. According to Monckton, during the battle, he had his horse shot from under him:

> *'...but charged on foot and beat Sir Hugh Bethel's Regiment of Horse, who was wounded and dismounted and my servant brought me his horse. When I was mounted upon him, the wind driving the smoke so as I could not see what became of the body that I commanded which went in pursuit of the enemy, I retired over a slow* [marsh] *where I saw a body of some 2000 horse that were broken which I endeavoured to rally.'*

He was later joined by Sir Marmaduke Langdale and they remained in the field until midnight when they were ordered, via a message from Rupert, to retire to York. Others, apart from Monckton, have remarked on the poor visibility:

> *'...the smoke of powder was so thick that we saw no light but what proceeded from the mouth of the guns.'*

It may have been possible, therefore for Monckton's band to remain undetected in the darkness.

The battle had lasted for just two hours. It had not been won at a stroke, with the wholesale collapse of one side. It had been a battle of several component encounters, separately fought, yet interdependent in nature. Cavalier resistance was ground down, remorselessly. There was no dramatic end to the fighting. It simply petered out in the darkness until all that remained were the groans of the wounded, the warm breeze which now dispersed the smoke still lingering oppressively in the moist night air – and the moon, its light strained through the shifting clouds, bathing the tableau of horror below in a pallid, spectral light.

Chapter 8

THE AFTERMATH

The flight of the Cavalier survivors to York was hampered by pursuing Roundhead horse, which harried them to 'within a mile of Yorke, cutting them downe so that their dead bodies lay three miles in length.' At Micklegate Bar, exhausted Cavaliers, begging for admission, were viewed coldly by Sir Thomas Glemham, who was prepared to admit only members of the garrison, allowing Rupert's men to fend for themselves. Sir Henry Slingsby reported: 'the whole street, up the bar, was thronged with wounded and lame soldiers; which made a pitiful cry among them.'

Rupert arrived at about 11.00 pm. According to his supporters, he had been cornered by the enemy and had 'killed 4 or 5 with his owne hands, and at last hee brake strongly through them.' Roundhead accounts place him in hiding until darkness falls, when he manages to acquire a stray horse and effect his escape hatless and in headlong flight. In any event, he succeeded in persuading Glemham to admit most of his troops to the city where all passed a most anxious night.

They need not have worried because Manchester's army, itself in some disarray, remained on the field that night and all the next day to bury the dead and provide for the wounded. The survivors, said Manchester:

having drained the weels to the mud, were necessitated to drinke water out of the ditches and out of places puddled with the horse feet... very few of the common souldiers did eate above the quantity of a penny loafe, from Tuesday till Saturday morning; and had no beere at all.'

The delay gave Rupert and Newcastle the opportunity they needed to escape, and both left York on the morning of 3 July.

The Siege of York was not resumed until the following day. Glemham had taken advantage of the breathing space afforded him to import fresh supplies – a task he accomplished by pillaging the local countryside of whatever he could find. Ignoring a demand 'to yeeld within 6 houres', the garrison set about strengthening the defences, in the hope that Rupert, refreshed

A Victorian artist's impression of the scene in York on 2 July 1644 as crowds lined the walls to witness the departure of Newcastle's troops.

and reinforced, would return to its aid. Glemham also dashed off a letter to the king, begging him for help. The Roundheads evidently thought that Glemham would try to hold out, for they went to the trouble of erecting new batteries, with which they began to pound the city. By 11 July, they were ready to storm the walls.

Before committing themselves, they gave Glemham one last chance to surrender. To their surprise, he agreed to enter into negotiations. Rupert apparently did not intend to return, Charles was not in a position to send more troops and Glemham's own weakened force of a few hundred men could not possibly hope to withstand any concerted attack. Mindful also of the potential horrors of an army of Scots on the rampage in the city, he had decided to bow out gracefully.

The negotiations themselves, which took place over the weekend of 13-15 July, resulted in generous terms of surrender. The garrison was allowed to march out armed and with colours flying; no Cavalier was to be plundered or offered 'injurie or affront'; at least two-thirds of the replacement Roundhead garrison was to be made up of Yorkshire men; in York itself, it was agreed 'That no building be defaced, nor any plundering, nor taking of any mans person, or of any part his Estate...' should occur.

To guarantee the safety of Glemham's departing troops, they were provided with an escort 'to Skipton, or the next Garrison Towne within sixteene miles of the Princes [Rupert's] army.' The escort was to comprise 'a Troop of Horse out of every of the three [allied] Armies.' This turned out to be more of a curse than a blessing for, on the first day out, the escort fell to plundering the Cavaliers and their supplies. The culprits were not, as Glemham had feared, the Scots, but men from the contingents of Manchester and Fairfax.

In York, Manchester, Fairfax and Leven were able to inform the Committee of Both Kingdoms that:

> 'the city of York is now reduced to the obedience of the King and Parliament... The Marquis of Newcastle's army being now reduced to nothing and Prince Rupert's forces being much weakened.'

This done, the allies parted company and headed for home ground – Leven marching north, and Manchester returning to Lincolnshire, while the Fairfaxes remained in Yorkshire. It was, in truth, impossible for them to stay together. As Manchester observed:

> *'The great necessities that the Scotch army and mine were in hath caused us to divide our armies and to march into fresh quarters... My men through want of clothes and other necessities fall sick daily.'*

In a pitiable condition they may have been, but at least they were alive. In excess of 4,000 bodies were interred on and in the near vicinity of the battlefield. In addition, there are the victims of the flight to York to take into account and the casualties who were likely to die from untended wounds – putting the final death toll in the region of 6,000. In some cases, relatives of the fallen would be informed of their loss. Thus, on 5 July 1644, Cromwell would write, somewhat bluntly, to his brother-in-law, Colonel Valentine Walton:

> *'Sir, God hath taken away your eldest son by a cannon-shot. It brake his leg. We were necessitated to have it cut off, whereof he died.'*

With reference to the loss of his own son, Oliver Jnr, who had died of smallpox while serving at Newport Pagnell in Buckinghamshire, Cromwell continued:

> *'Sir, you know my own trials this way: but the Lord supported me with this... There is your special child full of glory, never to know sin or sorrow any more. He was a gallant young man, exceedingly gracious. Before his death he was so full of comfort that he could not express it...'*

One wonders how 'full of comfort' young Walton really could have been, given the rudimentary nature of surgery. After the Battle of Edgehill, the King had increased the number of his personal physicians, while Parliament had made more general emergency provisions, but medical attention in the field was still scant. Although someone seems to have been on hand to dress Cromwell's neck wound, the more seriously injured stood little chance. Cornet Gabriel Ludlow, for example, died on the battlefield in agony 'with his belly broken and bowels torn.' Those of the wounded who survived long enough to be taken by cart to York were treated in makeshift 'hospitals' set up in a variety of locations, such as the *King's Manor* and the *Olde Starre Inn*. Here, limbs would be hacked off fully conscious individuals by surgeons and their mates, employed at rates of four shillings (20p) and two shillings and sixpence (12½p) respectively per day.

In 1644, many of the common soldiers who died in battle were

This illustration from a contemporary pamphlet shows Rupert in hiding, while the enemy ransacks his baggage train to reveal several artefacts attesting to his 'papist' leanings.

not even statistics; they merely ceased to exist. Some families, although well connected, were no more fortunate than the poor in their efforts to trace missing loved ones. Mary, the daughter of Sir Francis Trappes and wife to Colonel Charles Townley, a Cavalier killed at Marston Moor, is said to have been accosted by Cromwell while searching for her husband's body among the piles of naked corpses on the battlefield. Cromwell, fearful that she might be molested, had her escorted from the place. Mary, who died at the age of ninety-one, often repeated the story during her lifetime.

Often, the bereaved would learn of the loss of fathers, husbands, sons and brothers only through their failure to return. Of the anguish and suffering of those who survived the rigours of surgery, only hints appear in the lists of petitions for pensions. There was Robert Hughes of Cheshire, maimed with a poleaxe; Edmund Sudell of Lancashire, blinded and awarded an annual pension of ten shillings (50p); Thomas Cave of Northamptonshire, also blinded and, according to Cromwell, who interested himself in the man's case, 'in a very sad and perishing condition.' In 1648, at Cromwell's insistence, Cave was awarded the princely sum of £100.

Despite the carnage, over 100 Cavalier officers – including Sir Charles Lucas and Sir George Goring – and 2,000 men were taken prisoner. The booty included 28 cannon, 130 barrels of powder, 3 tons of bullets, 10,000 arms, several thousand pounds in gold and silver and 20 cart loads of cheese. Some of the Cavaliers' colours were torn to shreds by the Roundhead rank and file, but over one hundred were taken – Rupert's being 'nearly five yards square, with the arms of the Palatinate and a red cross in the middle.'

The Cavalier losses meant that, for practical purposes, Newcastle's Army of the North was no more. Newcastle himself made for Scarborough where Sir Hugh Cholmley managed to find a ship to take him to Hamburg and into exile for the next sixteen years. Some Cavaliers laid the blame for the defeat at Marston Moor squarely on Newcastle's shoulders, but the King never did. Later in the year, Charles would write:

'Right trusty and entirely beloved cousin and councillor we greet you well. The misfortune of our forces in the North we know is resented as sadly by you as the present hazard of the loss of so considerable a portion of this our kingdom deserves: which also affects us all the more, because in that loss so great a proportion falls upon yourself, whose loyalty and eminent merit we have ever held, and shall still, in a very high degree of our royal esteem.' A great proportion of the loss had, indeed, fallen upon Newcastle who, like many another prominent Cavalier, had ruined himself in the King's service.

At fifty, Newcastle was worn out by the personal and professional responsibilities of command, while Rupert, still only twenty-five, continued to be driven by the energy and impetuosity of youth. To all intents and purposes a foreign mercenary, Rupert had no ties to any part of the country and enjoyed the luxury of always being able to move on. From York, he marched his depleted forces to Thirsk and from there to Richmond, where he was met by Montrose. Neither could afford to offer the other any help, Montrose reporting ruefully:

'The Prince when we came to him took all the force from us and would supply us with none. So we were left abandoned...'

Abandoned pack horse
found in this area

upposed site of
Bean field

The western edge of Wilstrop Wood, where Rupert is said to have hidden in a 'bean field'. (OS Explorer 290 487536). His pack horse was found abandoned in the wood the day after the battle

Rupert continued on a roundabout route to Chester, arriving on 25 July and from where he turned his attention to recruiting in Wales – one of the last remaining Cavalier strongholds. He too, still enjoyed the support of the King, who wrote:

> *'As concerning your generositye & particular Fidelity & Friendship to me, I have an emplicit faith in you; this at all tymes shall be made good by your loving Oncle & faithfull frend, Charles R.'*

Scarborough Castle was governed by Sir Hugh Cholmley, who held it for Parliament before defecting to the King in March 1643

Clearly, Charles felt that he could afford to be generous as far as both Newcastle and Rupert were concerned. On 5 July, he had been at Evesham, where he received a note 'from Newark, implying that Prince Rupert had on Tuesday before utterly defeated the Scots, Fairfax and Manchester's Armys before York.' This despatch had been prepared somewhat prematurely, upon the initial collapse of the Roundhead right wing. Thus the truth, when it did surface, came as a doubly cruel blow.

If blame is to be apportioned, then it has to lie with Rupert as commander-in-chief. He had been truculent with Newcastle, he had not chosen the most auspicious moment for giving battle and, most significantly, instead of directing operations, he had assumed the role of a cavalry commander, restricting his attention to his own right wing.

To some extent, the enormity of the defeat was masked by good news elsewhere, in particular by a stunning Cavalier victory at Cropredy Bridge in Oxfordshire on 29 June. Yorkshire, thought Charles, was redeemable, but in this belief he was sadly mistaken. Only a handful of Cavalier fortresses continued to hold out. From Skipton Castle, Sir John Mallory was able to raid Thornton and Keighley, from Scarborough Castle, Sir Hugh Cholmley's cavalry, 200 strong, made a number of sorties and, from Pontefract Castle, Sir John Redman was able to send out 100 musketeers on raids behind enemy lines. Yet, in reality, such strongholds were little more than isolated prisons, where the Cavaliers remained conveniently bottled up.

In effect, Yorkshire was exhausted. The wool trade had been severely disrupted and in Leeds, grass was soon growing in the streets. In York, the Fosse had become unnavigable and trade 'become very mean and inconsiderable', the city's wealth

The Church of All Saints in Long Marston dates from the early fifteenth century. There are no records prior to 1648, but burials in the church or the churchyard did take place after the battle. Colonel Charles Fairfax, brother to Sir Thomas, who died from his wounds within the week, was interred here.

'reduced to a narrow scantling.' Scarborough's town and harbour had been plundered, ships rotted on the beach and the flour mills had been pulled down. At Hull, the sluice gates had been raised and the Humber banks cut, causing considerable flood damage to the surrounding agricultural land. The Cavaliers would enjoy future minor victories in the south and west, while in Scotland, Montrose had yet to embark on his series of famous marches. For the Yorkshire Cavaliers. however, the war was all but over, and many influential men followed Newcastle's example by fleeing overseas.

For the Roundhead commanders, Marston Moor brought mixed fortunes. If contemporary propaganda is to be believed, they were heroes all. Manchester was allocated 'a principal share in the victory', while Sir Thomas Fairfax 'redeemed his credit' and Cromwell 'changed the fortune of the day.' Thursday 18 July was proclaimed as a Day of Thanksgiving, and Puritan congregations throughout the land indulged themselves in interminably turgid sermons in which the Cavaliers were likened to 'the flesh-pots of Egypt', rejoicing in 'excess of wine, in revelling, banqueting, lasciviousness and lawless lusts.'

In fact, Leven and Fairfax Snr never fully recovered from the stigma of having deserted the battlefield. Although Sir Thomas Fairfax's reputation as a commander had not emerged quite intact, it was he who would be made General of the New Model Army. Some argued that he was merely Cromwell's stooge, appointed as '.....a Man of no quickness of Parts, of no Elocution, of no suspicious plotting Wit, and therefore One that Cromwell

Sir William Waller was an able Roundhead general whose defeat at Cropredy Bridge on 29 June 1644 was much overrated by the King. Cromwell later fought with Waller, as his subordinate, in the West country.

A Victorian artist's impression of victorious Roundhead cavalry regrouping for the pursuit of the vanquished foe.

could make use of at his pleasure.' Such claims cannot be dismissed out of hand. Fairfax may have been his own man but, as Cromwell was shrewdly aware, he was not an ambitious one.

The man who ultimately gained most from Marston Moor was Cromwell himself. His severest critics suggest that he played little part in the victory. According to Rogers, 'The memorial erected on the battlefield ascribes the chief credit for the victory to Oliver Cromwell, but there does not seem to be any evidence to support this claim.' An account of the battle penned by the Scot, Sir James Lumsden, is more measured:

'Our left wing of horss which was commandit by Livetennant Generall Cromwell and General major David Leslie caryed themselffs bravelie, and under God was ane main occasioun for our victorie. I must not overpass Manchester's foot, who did good service under the command of Generall major Crawford.'

This latter assessment conforms to the view that it was Cromwell's initial breakthrough, consolidated by Leslie, together with the character displayed by Crawford's infantry, that won the day. Without the Scots, and in the absence of infantry support, there may well have been no victory, yet Cromwell, the master of seventeenth century spin, helped himself to the lion's share of the credit – while being sufficiently gracious to acknowledge a little encouragement from the Almighty:

'The Left wing which I commanded being our own horse, saving a few Scots in our rear, beat all the Prince's horse. God made them as stubble to our swords.'

With Cromwell's rise to political power, it was inevitable that the myth that Marston Moor was his triumph and his alone, would develop into established fact.

TOUR 1

EXPLORING MARSTON MOOR

The battlefield of Marston Moor can be approached from York via the city's ring road, the A1237. Take the B1224 to Rufforth and Long Marston. At the Long Marston crossroads, turn right into Marston Lane. From the A1 to the west, take the Wetherby Racecourse exit which leads via York Road to Bilton. Just before Bilton, take the left turn to Tockwith. There is an exit from the A1 to the north of Wetherby which offers a direct route to Long Marston via Cowthorpe (OS Explorer 289 4252) and Tockwith but this is a narrow road and not quite so easily negotiated.

Ordnance Survey Explorer 289 and 290 are the relevant maps. Unfortunately, as luck would have it, the eastern half of the battlefield is on Explorer 290 and the western portion on 289. To avoid struggling with what at times resemble a pair of wayward bed sheets, I would recommend the old Ordnance Survey Pathfinder 664, which has the

The monument to the Battle of Marston Moor, standing at the corner of Moor Lane, was errected in 1936 by the Cromwell Association and the Harrogate group of the Yorkshire Archaeological Society. An illustrated plan of the battle is situated to the rear. (see page 65)

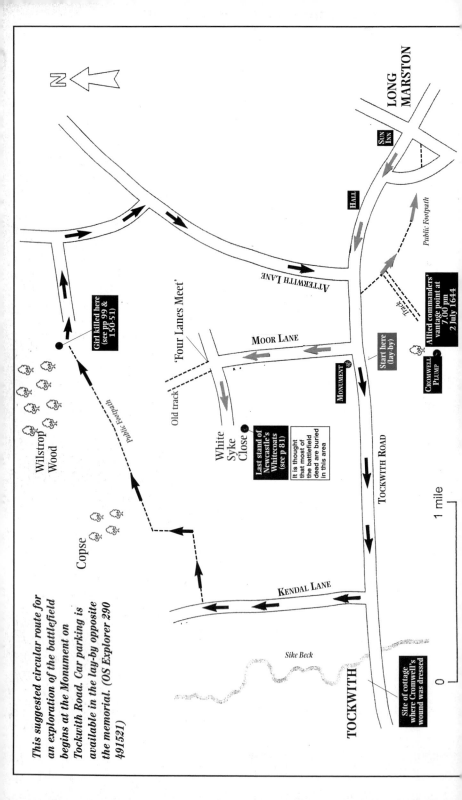

This suggested circular route for an exploration of the battlefield begins at the Monument on Tockwith Road. Car parking is available in the lay-by opposite the memorial. (OS Explorer 290 491521)

N

LONG MARSTON

Sun Inn

Hall

Public Footpath

Allied commanders' vantage point at 7.00 pm 2 July 1644

Cromwell Plump

Start here (lay-by)

Monument

Moor Lane

'Four Lanes Meet'

Attterwith Lane

track

Old track

Girl killed here (see pp 99 & 150-51)

Public Footpath

Wilstrop Wood

Copse

White Syke Close

Last stand of Newcastle's Whitecoats (see p 81)

It is thought that most of the battlefield dead are buried in this area

Tockwith Road

Kendal Lane

1 mile

0

Sike Beck

TOCKWITH

Site of cottage where Cromwell's wound was dressed

Public footpath leading from Kendal Lane (OS Explorer 289 475532), to the north of the Cavalier right wing. Byron's cavalry were turned and pushed back across the route of your walk. The hedge on the right, together with most of the other hedges which now dominate the landscape is a feature created by the enclosure movement in 1792.

Line of retreat of Byron's cavalry

battlefield in its entirety on one side of a single sheet. You should be able to complete the walk without the map. However, a sketch of the battle plan made on an overhead projection transparency and placed over the map would prove useful.

This suggested circular route begins at the Monument and heads west towards Tockwith, turning right along Kendal Lane. Another lay-by is located along Tockwith Road, close to the village of Tockwith, while there is ample roadside parking in Tockwith itself. I prefer to use the monument lay-by. Until quite recently, there was only a little rough off-road parking space here, but a new lay-by has been provided. Suggestions for a more substantial car parking area failed to gain planning approval. While a number of major battlefields such as Bosworth, Hastings, Bannockburn and Culloden do have visitor centres, Marston Moor does not, and the provision of such a facility here would constitute an invaluable addition to the list.

The monument – an imposing enough structure in itself – seems to lose something in terms of grandeur by standing on low lying land. It

Public footpath turns to the left at this point (OS Explorer 290 481532). Prince Rupert's rear lines comprising Widdrington, Porter and Rupert's Lifeguard were situated to the south of the ditch in the open ground beyond the gap in the hedge.

Continuation of the public footpath which veers off to the north east before the copse. Arrows indicate the line of the Cavalier retreat. (OS Explorer 290 481536).

is a relatively new addition to the landscape, having been erected in 1936 by the Cromwell Association and the Harrogate group of the Yorkshire Archaeological Society. An inscription on the monument gracefully acknowledges Leslie's assistance in Cromwell's rout of Byron's cavalry. To the rear of the monument is a mounted plan of the battle which is worth studying before setting out. It is fairly generalised in its depiction of troop deployments, but quite acceptable to all but those purists whose desire for accuracy borders upon paranoia.

Almost opposite the monument is Cromwell Plump, easily distinguishable by the tree with which it is crowned. From the monument, walk along the road towards Tockwith. To your left, on the high ground, was ranged the allied foot and to your right, the Cavalier infantry. A useful reference point is Marston Grange, the farm on the right, some 600 metres from the monument. Most sources place Crawford's infantry to your left, although opinions of the Cavalier deployment vary. The monument battle plan, for example, places Napier's musketeers to the right. John Barratt puts Byron and Rupert here, while Leadman suggests the infantry of O'Neil. David Smurthwaite puts Trevor's horse in the area now occupied by the farm buildings.

As you walk along, note how the ground to your left gradually levels out. Unlike Sir Thomas Fairfax on the right wing, Cromwell enjoyed a gentle slope to facilitate his cavalry charge. To your left, 400 metres beyond Marston Grange, is Bilton Bream, scene of the preliminary skirmish in which the Cavaliers tried to establish a foothold there early in the day.

Although it did not exist at the time of the battle, Kendal Lane is another useful reference point, roughly marking Byron's position on the Cavalier right wing. The existence of a tract of high ground, 'Rye Hill', nominated by some writers as the location of Tuke's regiment on the extreme right, is not immediately apparent. Walk up Kendal Lane, past the cottages on your left, until you reach the public footpath on the right – marked with an arrow and running along a hedge-lined ditch. Follow the line of the ditch to the end of the field, a distance of 500 metres. When you reach a footbridge crossing the ditch, turn sharp left. Follow the path, turning right to follow the hedgerow before reaching the copse ahead. The path now runs on a straight course to Wilstrop Wood.

You are now behind the Cavalier lines and although the hedgerows obscure much of the surrounding landscape, one is struck by the vastness of the battlefield – a daunting scenario for Yorkshiremen whose experience was limited to such cut-and-thrust skirmishes as Wetherby, Sherburn and Selby. Wilstrop Wood, now planted with conifers, must have covered a much wider area than it does today. On its western outskirts lay the 'beanfield' in which Rupert is alleged to have taken cover. As Newman as pointed out, the moor was not under cultivation and, if Rupert hid at all, then it must have been within the

Site of old cottage

Approximate site of gate where girl was trampled by retreating Cavalier horse.

Present day enclosure at the north-east corner of Wilstrop Wood (OS Explorer 290 494542) – a line of retreat for many Cavalier horse. The track leading to White Syke Bridge and Atterwith Lane is on the far side.

wood. Walk alongside the wood to its easternmost point. Leadman calculates that this spot marks the gate where a servant girl was killed as she opened a gate for the fleeing Cavaliers.

Walk through the open gateway ahead and through the small enclosure. As you emerge at the other side, you will see a single-track road to your right. Take this track which runs to White Syke Bridge. From end to end, retreating cavalry and infantry would have cut across your path at right angles, At the termination of the track, turn right onto what is quite a busy road, which does, however, have a wide negotiable grass verge. It ends in a T-Junction, where you should turn right again onto the not-so-busy Atterwith Lane. Leadman notes that many 'relics' were unearthed in the vicinity of Fox Covert – the copse on your left, 1,000 metres from the T-Junction. This also marks Goring's position – straddling Atterwith Lane – on the Cavalier left wing.

Continue walking to the end of Atterwith Lane and turn to the right. A little way along, on the left is a public footpath sign. Take this path, which runs to the rear of the houses bordering Marston Lane. The farm track which runs at right angles from the footpath is representative of the route taken by Sir Thomas Fairfax for his tricky descent prior to launching his assault on Goring's lines. If you walk up this track, it will lead you to the lower reaches of Cromwell Plump and to the view of the battlefield enjoyed by the allied generals. Return to the public footpath and follow it to emerge on Wetherby Road – the B1224. Turn to the left and walk up to Marston Lane, crossing the road for optional refreshment at *Sun Inn*.

From the inn, walk up Marston Lane. On your right is Marston Hall. Continue walking back to the monument. Running to the right of the monument is Moor Lane, a rough track dissecting the battlefield. Walk up this track and, at a distance of 400 metres from the road, you will see a ditch running off to your left. It is tempting to think of this as marking the location of the broken ditch masking the Cavalier front line. A particular point of interest about the track is that it serves as a

Line of ditch leading off Moor Lane, looking west from Goring's position on the Cavalier left wing towards the position occupied by Tillier's infantry.

Marston Moor, from Parliamentarian Centre, looking due north

bridleway. In wet weather, horses' hooves sink to a depth of several inches. In fine weather, the heavy clay dries to the consistency of concrete. On one occasion, I walked up the track in brilliant sunshine, the ground resembling a cobblestone road. As I returned, it began to rain, and within minutes I was sinking to my ankles in mud. The showers of rain which preceded the battle proved 'no small inconvenience' to the allies, while down below, on the poorly drained moor, manoeuvrability of men and horses must have been severely compromised.

Continue walking to the head of Moor Lane, where 'Four Lanes Meet'. This site later assumed a symbolic significance for, in 1654, it was chosen as the rendezvous for Cavaliers planning to march on York. One grassy track goes off to the right, along which Newcastle's men marched from York. To the left, a much wider path beckons. If you follow this path, it will take you to White Syke Close – the large field which opens out in the middle distance. It was here that the 'Whitecoats' staged their heroic last stand.

All that remains is for you to retrace your steps to the monument. This is a demanding walk and can easily be divided up into more manageable proportions to be undertaken at a leisurely pace over the course of a week-end.

TOUR 2

EXPLORING YORK

This tour of Civil War York is constructed around an anti-clockwise perambulation of the city walls. Begin at Fishergate Postern at the junction of Fishergate and Piccadilly. Fifteenth century in origin, Fishergate Postern is an isolated, seemingly neglected structure, strangely at odds with its surroundings. Its medieval origins are apparent to the casual observer, and it is the only one of the surviving smaller gateways to remain unaltered.

Sketch map showing route of walk of York. Any town plan of York is recommended.

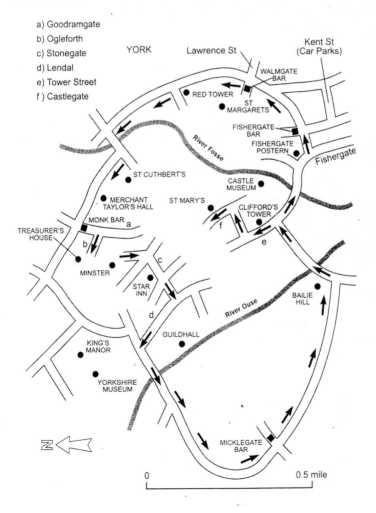

a) Goodramgate
b) Ogleforth
c) Stonegate
d) Lendal
e) Tower Street
f) Castlegate

YORK

Lawrence St

Kent St
(Car Parks)

WALMGATE BAR

RED TOWER

ST MARGARETS

FISHERGATE BAR

FISHERGATE POSTERN

Fishergate

River Fosse

ST CUTHBERT'S

CASTLE MUSEUM

MERCHANT TAYLOR'S HALL

ST MARY'S

CLIFFORD'S TOWER

MONK BAR

TREASURER'S HOUSE

MINSTER

STAR INN

BAILIE HILL

River Ouse

GUILDHALL

KING'S MANOR

YORKSHIRE MUSEUM

MICKLEGATE BAR

0   0.5 mile

The eastbound section of the wall is easily reached by stone steps which lead to a surprisingly narrow walkway. Follow the course of the wall to Fishergate Bar. It is no longer possible to walk through the Bars so descend to the road to rejoin the wall on the other side and continue to Walmgate Bar. All the medieval buildings beyond the bar, in Lawrence Street, were destroyed during the siege, including the hospital of St Nicholas and St Lawrence's Church. The latter was destroyed by artillery fire, the tower being the sole remaining portion of the original Norman structure. The damage was done from within the city for, by positioning guns in the churchyard, Sir Thomas Fairfax ensured that the church would constitute a legitimate target for the defenders' own artillery. Walmgate Bar itself suffered so severely that it had to be substantially rebuilt in 1648. Indentations left by cannon shot and bullets can be seen both here and at several additional places along the wall.

Beyond Walmgate, on the left, incongruous amid a modern blocks of flats, is St Margaret's Church. The physically fit can slip down from the wall at this point, while the more staid will have to descend from the Red Tower ahead and walk back. St Margaret's, closed and in a ruinous state, is of interest because of its twelfth century porch. Originally, the porch, carved with signs of the zodiac, was part of the medieval hospital of St Nicholas, in Lawrence Street. Beyond repair, following damage sustained during the siege, the hospital was torn down, but Sir Thomas Fairfax preserved the porch and arranged for it to be incorporated into St Margaret's.

The brick built Red Tower, dating from 1490, marks the beginning of a gap in the wall. The tower stood at what was the southern tip of an area of marshland known as the King's Fishpond, an expanse of water formed when the River Foss had been dammed during the construction of York Castle. From the Red Tower to Layerthorpe Postern, a distance of about a quarter of a mile, the Fishpond – in the absence of a wall – constituted the main line of defence. By the time of the siege, it had shrunk considerably. It still seems to have proved an effective barrier although, following the Battle of Marston Moor, Slingsby states that the Roundheads:

'made a bridge to clap over the Fosse and store of hurdles for a storm, where by the Laterne [Layerthorpe] Posterne it was most easy, having nothing but the ditch, with drought almost dry, for to hinder their entrance.'

Walk along Foss Islands Road, crossing the river via Layerthorpe Bridge. Directly ahead is Peasholme Green. Along here on the right is St Cuthbert's Church, damaged during the siege. At the end of Peasholme Green, turn right into Aldwark to see St Anthony's Hall, used during the siege both as a hospital. Continue along Aldwark to Merchant Taylor's Hall, which saw service both as a hospital and an armoury.

he Souldiers in their passage to York turn unto reformers pull down Popish pictures, break down rayles, turn altars into Tables.

Roundhead troops were inveterate iconoclasts and desecrated many churches. It took the direct intervention of Sir Thomas Fairfax to ensure that the same did not happen to York Minster upon the Capitulation of the city.

At the end of Aldwark, cross Goodramgate to enter Ogleforth (to the right is Monk Bar, the scene of Rupert's departure after Marston Moor), walking round into Chapter House Street. Situated here is Treasurer's House which, after the Civil War, was owned for a time by Sir Thomas Fairfax. At the bottom of Chapter House Street to the left is College Street, site of St William's College, where Charles I established the Royal Mint in 1642. To the right is Minster Yard and York Minster. The Minster suffered little damage during the siege, although it was noted that, during services, the besiegers would make a:

> 'Hellish disturbance, by shooting against and battering the Church, in so much that sometimes a Cannon Bullet has come in at the windows, and bounc'd about... among the Pillars...'

Artillery was never mounted on The Minster, and so it was not, strictly speaking, a target, but it did appear to enjoy a divine protection of sorts, similar to that bestowed upon St Paul's Cathedral in the capital during the Second World War. In the aftermath of Marston Moor and the surrender of York, the intervention of the Fairfaxes undoubtedly saved The Minster from destruction. Probably the greatest stroke of fortune lay in the fact that the Cavaliers were on the inside and the Roundheads on the outside. Had the positions been reversed, it is likely that The Minster's fixtures and fittings would have been annihilated.

The Puritanical spleen was often vented in the wholesale destruction of stained glass windows. In this connection, a memorial situated in the Chapter House commemorates the contribution of the Fairfaxes towards the preservation of The Minster's priceless stained glass, both father and son having 'preserved from destruction the treasures of glass of York Minster.'

Interred in The Minster were the more celebrated casualties of the conflict. Of interest in this connection is the tomb of Archbishop John Dolben, in the south choir aisle. Dolben, an Oxford student, fought for the Cavaliers at Marston Moor and was wounded by a musket ball. He recovered sufficiently to participate in the defence of York during the renewal of the siege, when he was shot in the thigh. Overcoming this second wound, he returned to his studies. Forty years later, he was appointed Archbishop of York. Other Minster burials included Colonel Charles Slingsby, Colonel William Evers and Sir Philip Byron, younger brother of Lord Byron.

From Minster Yard on the south side of The Minster, walk across Petergate into Stonegate. In Stonegate stands *Ye Olde Starre Inn*, prominent by virtue of its 'gallows' sign spanning the narrow street. It is thought to be York's oldest public house. William Foster, landlord of the *Olde Starre* in 1644, supported the King. Following the garrison's capitulation, he was powerless to prevent his premises being invaded by Roundhead troopers who filled the large kitchen and, he complained, 'gamed and swore'. The inn's cellar was used to tend the

Sir Thomas Fairfax spent his last years confined to this wheelchair - an illustration of which appeared in Edmund Bogg's 'The Old Kingdom of Elmet' (1902).

All Saints, Pavement.

All Saints Church. A light burning in the tower guided travellers through the Forest of Galtres.

Marston Moor wounded, whose anguished cries still allegedly haunt the site.

At the bottom of Stonegate, walk across Davygate into St Helen's Square. Off the Square and backing on to the River Ouse is Guildhall. Some of the arms which Queen Henrietta Maria brought with her were stored here – too many, in fact, for the floor gave way under the weight. A stained glass window on an historical theme depicts the siege and also features Sir Thomas Fairfax. From St Helen's Square, walk up Lendal and cross Museum Street to enter Museum Gardens – originally the grounds of St Mary's Abbey. The Abbey stood outside the city wall which surrounds the public library. St Mary's had its own defensive wall stretching from St Mary's Tower – mined by the Roundheads in 1644 – to Bootham, and down to Bootham Bar. The Benedictine Abbey itself had been in a ruinous condition since the Dissolution of the Monasteries, but the Abbot's Palace became the residence of the Lord President of the Council of the North. The last incumbent of this office, abolished by Parliament in 1641, was Thomas Wentworth, Earl of Strafford, executed by Charles in an effort to appease his critics. To the rear of the Abbey is St Olave's Church, founded in 1055 but rebuilt in the eighteenth century as a result of extensive damage suffered during the siege, when one of the defenders' guns mounted on it exploded.

Cross the Ouse by Lendal Bridge to rejoin the wall on the west bank. At the extreme south west corner of the wall stand the remains of Sadler Tower, the destruction of which by cannon fire on the resumption of the siege appears to have been a significant factor in Glemham's decision to surrender. Follow the course of the wall around to Micklegate Bar, where Marston Moor's defeated Cavaliers clamoured for entry. Beyond the Bar, amid the nineteenth-century

Micklegate Bar, York in the seventeenth century.

urban sprawl, one can just make out the rise of the land towards the site of the Cavalier gun emplacements on The Mount sconce. Within, a visit to the Micklegate Bar Museum will be of interest.

Continue walking along the wall to its termination at Baile Hill, site of a Norman keep which probably predated Clifford's Tower. Both towers had been constructed of wood, but whereas the latter was subsequently rebuilt in stone, its sister tower had been abandoned. Prior to the siege, Baile Hill was strengthened and two cannon placed upon it.

Descending from the wall, cross the Ouse by Skeldergate Bridge and bear left into Tower Street for Clifford's Tower. This was the centrepiece of the city defences. Newcastle's abortive terms of surrender had stipulated that:

'Clifford's Tower (the chiefe Fort in Yorke) *be still kept Garrisoned by them* [the defenders] *until the Articles... be punctually performed.'*

Perhaps the most important museum as far as the Civil War is concerned is York Castle Museum which, among other exhibits, contains 'one of the most comprehensive collections of English Civil War armour in the country.'

From the Castle Museum, proceed up Castlegate, turning right into Coppergate and sharp left into Ousegate, site of the Church of All Saints. It is popularly known as the 'lantern' church. This is because a light was kept burning in the tower throughout the hours of darkness as a guide to travellers – including Rupert's army – approaching York from the north through the Forest of Galtres.

A right turn into Piccadilly, will bring you back to your starting point at Fishergate Postern.

TOUR 3

LOCAL INTEREST

Bilbrough (OS Explorer 290 5346)

The Bilbrough estate came into the possession of the Fairfax family in the early sixteenth century. The exterior of Bilbrough Manor (OS Explorer 290 529464) bears the date '1670' and Sir Thomas Fairfax's initials. A Norman church was demolished in the nineteenth century to make way for the present structure, erected by a later Thomas Fairfax. A chantry chapel, founded in 1492 and incorporated in the new building, contains the tomb of Sir Thomas Fairfax and his wife, Anne. The inscription on the tomb is supplemented by a memorial plaque erected by their daughter, Mary, describing Sir Thomas's career. It is rumoured that his body was afterwards removed and reburied in secret at Walton, near Wakefield, his friends being fearful that his remains might meet a similar fate to those of Cromwell.

St James' Church, Bilbrough, resting place of Sir Thomas Fairfax.

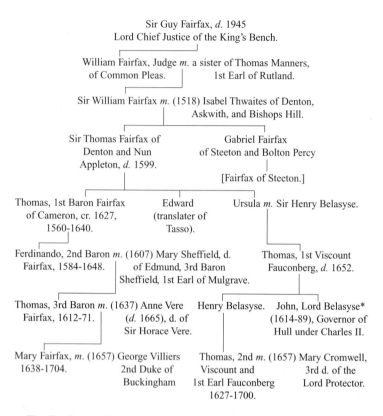

Sir Guy Fairfax, *d.* 1945
Lord Chief Justice of the King's Bench.

William Fairfax, Judge *m.* a sister of Thomas Manners,
of Common Pleas. 1st Earl of Rutland.

Sir William Fairfax *m.* (1518) Isabel Thwaites of Denton,
Askwith, and Bishops Hill.

Sir Thomas Fairfax of   Gabriel Fairfax
Denton and Nun   of Steeton and Bolton Percy
Appleton, *d.* 1599.

[Fairfax of Steeton.]

Thomas, 1st Baron Fairfax   Edward   Ursula *m.* Sir Henry Belasyse.
of Cameron, cr. 1627,   (translater of
1560-1640.   Tasso).

Ferdinando, 2nd Baron *m.* (1607) Mary Sheffield, d.   Thomas, 1st Viscount
Fairfax, 1584-1648.   of Edmund, 3rd Baron   Fauconberg, *d.* 1652.
Sheffield, 1st Earl of Mulgrave.

Thomas, 3rd Baron *m.* (1637) Anne Vere   Henry Belasyse.   John, Lord Belasyse*
Fairfax, 1612-71.   (*d.* 1665), d. of   (1614-89), Governor of
Sir Horace Vere.   Hull under Charles II.

Mary Fairfax, *m.* (1657) George Villiers   Thomas, 2nd *m.* (1657) Mary Cromwell,
1638-1704.   2nd Duke of   Viscount and   3rd d. of the
Buckingham   1st Earl Fauconberg   Lord Protector.
1627-1700.

The Fairfax family tree suggests that the privileged classes, regardless of political differences, remained a close-knit group. The daughters of Cromwell and Sir Thomas Fairfax both married into prominent Royalist families.

According to his poem, *Upon the Hill and Grove at Bill-borow*, Andrew Marvell was much taken with Bilbrough:

See how the arched Earth does here
Rise in perfect Hemisphere!
The stiffest Compass could not strike
A Line more circular and like;

It was claimed that the hill served as a landmark for ships entering the River Humber, and so Marvell continues:

How glad the weary Seamen hast
When they salute it from the Mast!
By Night the Northern Star their way
Directs, and this so less by Day.

Bolton Percy (OS Explorer 290 5341)

The Fairfax family acquired the Bolton Percy estate at the same time as they received Bilborough – Sir William Fairfax and Isabel Thwaites being married in All Saints Church, Bolton Percy in 1518. Ferdinando, Lord Fairfax is buried here, together with Henry Fairfax, rector during the Civil War, and Sir William Fairfax. Scoring on the oak stalls is said to have been caused by Roundhead troops sharpening their swords.

Cawood (OS Explorer 290 3757)

There has been a castle at Cawood since the tenth century. Its heyday was in the piping times of King Henry VIII. He stayed at Cawood with his young bride, Catherine Howard. After he had lost favour with Henry, Cardinal Wolsey made his home here. Cawood is frequently mentioned in the various accounts of the Civil War. Until 19 May 1644, when it was taken by Sir John Meldrum, it was held by the Cavaliers. Meldrum captured three guns and 200 soldiers, but lost 40 prisoners when, on 28 June, Cavaliers from Pontefract launched a surprise attack. In 1646, the castle was destroyed by order of Parliament, and only the majestic gateway tower has survived. The bridge of boats used by the Fairfaxes en route to York may have been constructed at the point occupied by the swing bridge which spans the Ouse today.

Healaugh (OS Explorer 290 4947)

The Earl of Leven's army marched via Healaugh in the afternoon on 2 July 1644 and were within a mile of Tadcaster when they received reports of Rupert's army beginning to gather on Marston Moor. The

Site of the cottage at Tockwith at which Cromwell's wound was dressed. The dwelling survived until 9 October 1945, when a Stirling Mark IV bomber from nearby RAF Marston Moor crashed into Tockwith's main street damaging several buildings - including the cottage, which was subsequently demolished.

The door of the Church of St John the Evangelist in Healaugh which, according to local tradition, still bears bullet holes made by a Roundhead trooper's carbine.

early Norman Church of St John the Evangelist has undergone much restoration work since the seventeenth century. Its door bears the marks of what are allegedly carbine shots. Apparently, the horse of a dragoon en route to Marston Moor cast a shoe and its rider stopped at the village smithy to have it replaced. The blacksmith was rather slow and the dragoon threatened to burn his house over his head. The smith replied that he might not have a chance to do so, upon which the dragoon discharged the contents of his carbine at the church door.

Moor Monkton (OS Explorer 290 5056)

Sir Henry Slingsby lived at Red House, a mile from the village on the banks of the River Ouse (OS Explorer 290 529571). Within recent years, Red House has seen service as a preparatory school although, at time of writing (2003), it is planned to convert it into a number of flats.

Nun Appleton (OS Explorer 290 5539)

A Cistercian convent was established here in 1150. Early in the sixteenth century, Sir William Fairfax of Steeton, High Sheriff of York, married a local heiress, Isabel Thwaites. Upon the death of her father, Thomas Thwaites of Denton, Isabel had been placed in the care of the Abbess of Nun Appleton, and Sir William found it necessary to abduct her. In 1540, during the dissolution of the monasteries, the convent was closed and twelve years later, by a quirk of fate, the land was given to Isabel's two sons, who built the first Nun Appleton Hall. The second Nun Appleton – of Sir Thomas Fairfax's time – had been planned by his grandfather, and was finally completed in 1651. This house was described as:

> 'a picturesque brick mansion with stone copings and a high steep roof, and consisted of a centre and two wings at right angles, forming three sides of a square facing to the north... A noble park, with splendid oak trees, and containing 300 head of deer, stretched away to the north; while on the south side were the ruins of the old nunnery, the flower garden and the low meadows called ings, extending to the banks of the Wharfe.'

It was this Nun Appleton which formed the subject of Marvell's *Upon Appleton House*, a poem of ninety-seven stanzas recounting the story of Sir William and Isabelle and extolling the beauty of the mansion and grounds. Marvell considered Nun Appleton the pick of his patron's residences:

> *Him Bishops-Hill, or Denton may,*
> *Or Bilbrough, better hold than they:*
> *But Nature here hath been so free*
> *As if she said leave this to me.*

A third house was the work of the Milner family. The eighteenth century gardens, listed by English Heritage, show no trace of their earlier plan, although the remains of the convent are still discernible.

Although RAF Marston Moor closed in 1945, much of its infrastructure is still intact, inlcuding these two T-2 hangars (OS Explorer 289 458528) once capable of housing 23 aircraft.

Poppleton (OS Explorer 290 5554)

It is difficult to pinpoint the site of the pontoon bridge erected by Manchester and used by Rupert to cross the Ouse. Peter Wenham places it at Clifton in the vicinity of the present day Water End crossing (OS Explorer 290 589528). At the other extreme, the Royal Commission on Historical Monuments publication on the City of York's defences suggests Poppleton, at the point indicated by the track to Overton on the west bank of the Ouse (OS Explorer 290 558552). The problem is that, according to Stockdale, Rupert crossed the river 'by the bridge they surprised the night before, and by a ford near to it.' There was a ford at Poppleton, and it may have been that both a pontoon at Clifton and a ford at Poppleton were involved. Slingsby, who lived locally and who was involved in the siege, states that 'The prince passed over at Poppleton where the Scots had made a bridge of boats'. If, as Slingsby also states, Rupert came 'within 3 or 4 miles of York, upon the forest side', this would place him in the vicinity of Poppleton, making it inevitable that he would encounter the dragoons left by Manchester to guard the makeshift bridge.

Skip Bridge (OS Explorer 290 4855)

By despatching some cavalry from Knaresborough, along the road to York, to Skip Bridge, Rupert convinced the allies that he intended to make a direct approach to York. 'New Skip Bridge' now spans the River Nidd as part of the A59. The old bridge, to the south, gives access to a car park/picnic area.

To visit the site of the medieval village of Wilstrop, walk from the car park about 400 metres along the A59 towards York. Turn down the track at the field boundary on your right, cross the railway line and bear to the right. The undulating ground constitutes the remains of the 'lost' village. Wilstrop had ceased to exist long before the Battle of Marston Moor was fought. Towards the end of the fifteenth century, the lord of the manor, Myles Willestrope, evicted the villagers and enclosed the common land in order to create a park for his house.

TOUR 4

FURTHER AFIELD

Despite the extent of the fighting in Yorkshire, there are – as the following list suggests – relatively few reminders of the Civil War. So many fortresses which had played an active role were deliberately slighted – Cawood, Helmsley, Knaresborough, Pontefract, Scarborough, Tickhill, Wressle – to prevent them falling into the hands of Royalist sympathisers. The hotly contested bridges at Wetherby, Tadcaster and Ferrybridge still remain, albeit in modern versions. Many of the battles which took place within the county were little more than skirmishes and we know them simply as names: Monk Fryston (10 December 1642), Stanley (21 May 1643), Kilham (10 February 1644), Driffield (13 April 1644), Halton (7 October 1644) and so on. They may have been small potatoes in comparison with the major battles, but they were still encounters in which men fought and died for 'the cause', whether it be for King or Parliament.

Adwalton Moor (OS Explorer 288 2228)
The centre of this battlefield approximates to the recreation ground on Moorside Road in Drighlington. Sir Thomas Fairfax occupied a position to the north of Warrens Lane (OS Explorer 288 219283) down which he fled towards Halifax. Warrens Lane is now a footpath which can be followed to Oakwell Hall Country Park. (In 1643, Oakwell Hall was owned by the Batt family. After the battle, the Cavaliers burst into the building during their pursuit of the fleeing Fairfax – much to the distress of Mrs Batt, who was ill in bed at the time.)

Helmsley Castle (OS Landranger 100 6083)
It was at the siege of Helmsley Castle that Sir Thomas Fairfax was seriously wounded, a musket ball shattering his shoulder. Sir Jordan Crosland, keeping Helmsley for the Cavaliers, held out for three months. There was still plenty of fight left in the Yorkshire Royalists for, on 4 November 1644, a joint relief party from Skipton and Knaresborough temporarily gained the upper hand by scattering the besiegers. The garrison itself made a number of sorties, in the process of which Fairfax sustained his wound. Although well supplied with ammunition, the defenders were starved into surrender on 22 November 1644. The Roundheads proudly took possession of the castle, nine pieces of ordnance, 300 muskets and pikes and six barrels of powder. Fairfax was later given the Helmsley estate as part-reward for his services, but its owner, the Duke of Buckingham, ensured its return by the expedient of marrying Fairfax's daughter, Mary. Helmsley Castle is now in the care of English Heritage and facilities include an exhibition on the castle's history.

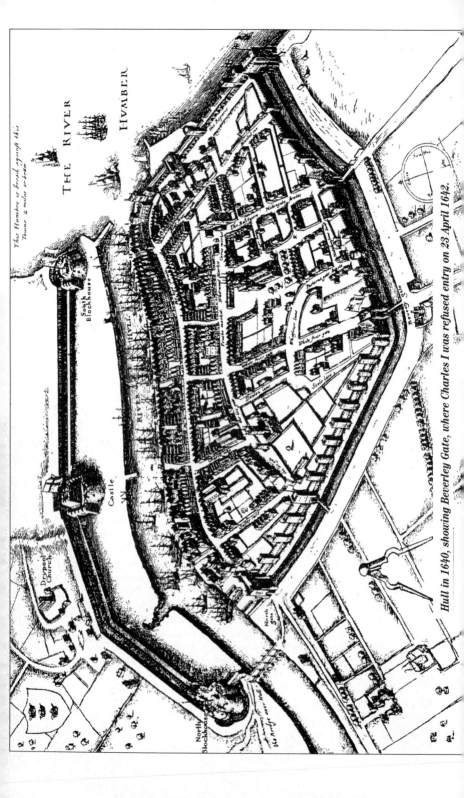

THE RIVER HVMBER

This Humber is forsed up with this Towne 2 miles or better

South Blockhouse

Castle

Drypool Church

North Blockhouse

North Gate

the bridge ov[er] Kelingrene

Hull in 1640, showing Beverley Gate, where Charles I was refused entry on 23 April 1642.

Howley Hall (OS Explorer 288 2525)

Howley was owned by Sir Thomas Saville. In June 1643, prior to the Battle of Adwalton, the hall was besieged by the Earl of Newcastle and pounded by 'Gog' and 'Magog', the heavy guns which were later captured by the Roundheads during Newcastle's siege of Hull. The garrison surrendered after ten days. At the end of the war, such damage as the hall had sustained was rectified. In the eighteenth century, the structure was demolished and all that remains are ruins by Howley Hall golf club, in an area crossed by several public footpaths.

Kingston Upon Hull

Visitors may view the excavated remains of Beverley Gate, main entrance to the old town, where Sir John Hotham famously barred the entry of King Charles I on 23 April 1642. The *Olde White Harte Inn*, complete with 'Plotting Chamber' where Hotham allegedly hatched his plans, still exists off Silver Street.

Excavated remains of Beverley Gate.

Sir John Hotham, Parliamentary Governor of Hull 1642-43, resented the power of the Fairfaxes and planned to change sides. Both he and his son were compromised by correspondence discovered in the Marquis of Newcastle's abandoned coach after Marston Moor.

Newburgh Priory (OS Landranger 100 5476)

Built on the site of an Augustinian Priory, Newburgh was the home of Thomas Bellasys, Lord Falconberg who married Oliver Cromwell's daughter, Mary. Legend has it that Mary had her father's head entombed in a secret chamber within the walls.

Norton Conyers Hall (OS Landranger 99 3176)

Norton Conyers is fourteenth century in origin – the house having been in the possession of the Graham family for nearly four hundred years. Sir Richard Graham fought for the Cavaliers at Marston Moor. Despite suffering from twenty-six wounds, Sir Richard made his way home and rode upstairs to bed. Leadman tells us that

'At Norton Conyers Hall there is to be seen in the present

staircase a portion of an old step, and on it is the distinct mark of a horse's shoe, which is said to have been made when Sir Richard rode upstairs to die.'

Pontefract Castle (OS Explorer 289 4622)

Pontefract Castle was secured for the King in 1642. In October of that year, Captain John Hotham made an unsuccessful attempt to capture it, and in December in became Newcastle's temporary headquarters. In June 1643, Queen Henrietta Maria stayed here en route between York and Oxford. Notwithstanding its importance, Pontefract Castle was not besieged until December 1644. The siege was lifted temporarily in March 1645, and the garrison surrendered in July 1645. Three years on, during the Second Civil War, Pontefract Castle was again secured for the King and withstood a siege which lasted six months, from 9 September 1648 to 24 March 1649. It was the last Cavalier stronghold in England to fall – Fairfax receiving another wound in the final siege.

In the wake of the Civil War, Parliament was responsible for slighting many fine castles and fortified houses. In the case of Pontefract, however, the citizens themselves petitioned Parliament for permission to carry out demolition, being of the opinion that the castle was the source 'of former miseries and future fears.' The remains of the Great Round Tower survive and a visitor centre contains a wealth of information to help one explore the site.

Ripley Castle (OS Landranger 99 2861)

Oliver Cromwell slept here (to coin a tired phrase) the night after Marston Moor in his quest for fleeing Cavaliers, and it was at Ripley that he had his celebrated encounter with 'Trooper' Jane Ingilby. Together with her brother, the head of the household, Sir William Ingilby, Jane fought for the King at Marston Moor. After the battle, they reached home safely, but then Cromwell – engaged in hunting down fleeing Cavaliers – appeared, seeking a night's rest. Sir William spent the evening lodged in a secret chamber while Cromwell slept on a chair in the Library, under the supervision of Jane who was armed with a brace of pistols. She said she needed two pistols because she was more accustomed to handling a sword. Many years ago, the late Sir Joslan Ingilby told a slightly different version. In his account, it was Sir William's wife who sat nursing a pair of pistols while Cromwell slept. On his departure, Cromwell had posed the question, 'Why two pistols?', to which Lady Ingilby replied, 'I might have missed with the first.' While the former version may be the more accurate, my own preference is for the latter.

Upon his departure, Cromwell executed several prisoners against the Gatehouse wall. His men had been lodged in Ripley's All Saints Church, where more prisoners were stood against the east gable wall and shot. The impression of musket balls can be seen in the walls at both locations.

Seacroft Moor (OS Explorer 289 3637)

Seacroft is now a suburb of Leeds, but some of the moorland, bearing the name 'Whinmoor', survives. On his march from Tadcaster, Sir Thomas Fairfax had managed to hold Goring's Cavaliers at bay while crossing the expanse of Bramham Moor (OS Explorer 289 4442) by using his cavalry to cover the flanks of the infantry. As Seacroft Moor was 'much less' than Bramham, the foot grew more confident, dispersing into 'houses, where they sought for drink', and were overtaken by the enemy cavalry. A little to the north east of the Moor is Kiddal Hall (OS Explorer 289 3939). The owner, John Ellis, a Cavalier, was killed by the Roundheads as they scoured the area for sustenance and his ghost allegedly still hovers around the old house.

Scarborough Castle

Held for the King by Sir Hugh Cholmeley, Scarborough Castle was under siege from 18 February to 25 July 1645. The curtain wall, barbican and ruined Norman keep survive under the care of English Heritage. A sally port and flight of steps leading to the South Steel battery, constructed on Cholmeley's instructions to protect the harbour, also remain. Before the castle lie the ruins of the old tower of St Mary's Church. Sir John Meldrum, besieging the castle, sited some of his artillery within the church – return fire from the castle causing sufficient damage to lead to the tower's collapse in 1659.

Selby

Selby was the scene of more than one encounter between Cavaliers and Roundheads, fought within an old town street pattern which survives largely unchanged. The battle preceding the Siege of York occurred on the west bank of the Ouse, between the houses and the river. At the end of The Quay stood the old ferry stage where the Cavaliers' bridge of boats would have been situated. During the Civil War, Selby Abbey suffered some damage at the hands of the Fairfaxes and it is said that they even used it for stabling horses.

Sherburn-in-Elmet (OS Explorer 290 4933)

Sir Thomas Fairfax provided some infuriatingly sketchy accounts of the battles in which he was engaged. However, from his account of the Sherburn-in-Elmet raid, we can identify the 'pass', by which he and his then comrade-in-arms Captain John Hotham, approached the village, as Cross Moor Bridge on Moor Lane. The parish church on Church Hill would have been the vantage point from which the Cavaliers espied Sir Thomas's approach, and their 'barricado' may have been situated at some point between Sir John's Lane and the lower village.

Site of pontoon
bridge

The Battle of Selby (11 April 1644) was to prove crucial to the outcome of the Civil War in Yorkshire. The Fairfaxs' defeat of Sir John Belasyse left York exposed, leading to the siege of York and, in turn, to Marston Moor. Cavalier survivors of the Selby encounter made good their escape by means of a pontoon bridge spanning the River Ouse at the end of The Quay.

Wakefield

Wakefield is better known for its association with the Wars of the Roses than with the Civil War. In the Battle of Wakefield of 21 May 1643, Sir Thomas Fairfax assaulted the town via Norgate (Northgate)

The Old Church, Wentworth, burial place of the Earl of Strafford.

Sandal Castle, Wakefield, now has a visitor's centre and the castle mound has an observation platform.

and Wrengate (Warrengate). The Cavalier defenders were cleared from their barricades, along with three troops of horse in the Market Place. Lord Goring was taken prisoner and Parliament made much of what was in reality a minor affair, styling it 'a miraculous victory.'

Wakefield's Sandal Castle (OS Landranger 110 3318) was one of several Cavalier strongholds which, following the Marston Moor defeat, were left to their own devices, no concerted effort being made to reduce them until 1645. Sandal had been in a ruinous condition for many years before the outbreak of war and it had been necessary to bolster the decaying defences with a series of earthworks. The first siege, in April 1645, undertaken by Sir John Savile, was quickly terminated as a result of a well orchestrated sortie by the garrison. A second blockade in June was lifted voluntarily. In September, however, Colonel Robert Overton arrived with four heavy guns and, within three weeks, had pounded Sandal into submission. On 1 October 1645, the garrison commander, Colonel George Bonivant, surrendered. A newly opened (2002) visitor centre at Sandal Castle traces the castle's history.

Wentworth (OS Landranger 111 9838)

Thomas Wentworth, the Earl of Strafford, occupied a house which was subseqently incorporated into the present day Wentworth Woodhouse. Strafford served Charles I faithfully as chief advisor until 1641, when his master sent him to block in an effort to appease his critics. The Earl lies buried in the Old Church in the village.

TOUR 5

RUPERT'S ROUTE

To follow the route of Prince Rupert's relief march through Yorkshire, begin at Gisburn (OS Landranger 103 8248) which, prior to county boundary changes, enjoyed the privilege of being situated in Yorkshire. Cromwell, too, would pass through Gisburn, staying at Gisburn Park on 15 August 1648 before the Battle of Preston, his men – according to the usual reports – stabling their mounts in the Church of St Mary the Virgin and breaking the stained glass windows.

From Gisburn, take the A59 eastbound. At Thornton-in-Craven (OS Landranger 103 9048) stood the Manor House belonging to Sir William Lister, whose daughter, Frances, was married to John Lambert. In April 1643, Colonel Conyers Darcy's assault on the Manor was repelled by Lambert's dragoons. A second attempt, made in July 1643, was more successful, and although Darcy's Cavaliers took possession of the Manor, they themselves were ejected within a few days. It is said that many years after the Manor's destruction by Rupert, excavations revealed one of the rooms, with its furnishings undisturbed.

Continue along the A59 to Skipton and Skipton Castle (OS Landranger 103 9952). Although slighted in 1648, the castle was

Rupert rested his army at Skipton Castle and sent messengers to York to inform the garrison of his approach.

tastefully restored ten years later by Lady Anne Clifford. From Skipton, take the A59 to Bolton Bridge (Landranger 104 0752) where Rupert's cavalrymen grazed their horses. Take the B6160 to Addingham. To the east, beyond the Wharfe, is Howber Hill (Landranger 104 0952), where Rupert is said to have thrown up a defensive earthwork. From Addingham (Landranger 104 0749) take the A65 to Ilkley (OS Landranger 104 1147). Cross the Wharfe and follow Denton Road eastbound to Denton Park (Landranger 104 1448), home of the first Lord Fairfax and birthplace of his grandson, Sir Thomas. The Denton estates were acquired by the Fairfax family in 1518, with the marriage of Sir William Fairfax and Isabel Thwaites. The original house was destroyed by fire, no trace of it surviving in the structure which stands today.

Return to Ilkley and follow the A65 to Otley (OS Landranger 104 2044). Continue through Otley on the A660. Above Otley is Farnley Hall and the remains of Farnley Wood (Landranger 104 2147) – the wood providing refuge for fleeing Cavaliers after Marston Moor. In 1663, the site was the focus of the Farnley Wood Plot. The plotters, a motley assortment of Nonconformists and veterans of the New Model Army, planned to march on York as a first step to deposing Charles II. The scheme, which failed, is often cited as the final act in the tragedy of the English Civil Wars. Fairfax, who had been approached to lead the conspirators, took the trouble to beg for leniency to be shown to the ringleaders. His pleas went unheard and eighteen were executed.

Beyond Otley, at the junction with the A658, take the latter road northbound to Knaresborough and Knaresborough Castle (Landranger 104 3456). According to local legend, Cromwell dined here the night before the battle of Marston Moor. This is rather unlikely as Knaresborough had been a Cavalier stronghold since the beginning of the war. Sir Henry Slingsby luxuriated in the title 'Vigilator and Janitor' of the castle yet, interestingly enough, it was garrisoned, not by Yorkshiremen, but by troops recruited from far and wide – including London – whose preferred function was to terrorise the surrounding countryside. After Marston Moor, matters had to be taken more seriously and the castle was besieged from 22 August 1644. A concerted effort to take it was not made until the following December when Roundhead artillery breached the walls, forcing the garrison comprising one hundred and forty-six men to surrender. In 1648, much of the fabric was destroyed by order of Parliament, except the Courthouse and the King's Tower which was allowed to remain so that it could serve as a prison. The Courthouse Museum houses a Civil War gallery. Its collection includes the bloodstained shirt worn by Sir Henry Slingsby for his execution. In the Church of St John the Baptist in Church Lane, is the Slingsby Chapel, containing monuments to the family of that name, including Sir Henry Slingsby's tomb.

From Knaresborough, take the A6055 to Boroughbridge (Landranger 99 3967). At the roundabout on the north bank of the River Ure, take the minor road to Milby and Brafferton. At Milby (Landranger 99 403679) Rupert could have swung eastwards to effect a crossing of the River Swale at Myton (Landranger 99 4366). The present-day bridge is about 200 yards (183 metres) above the site of an old wooden structure. However, he chose to march a further 3 miles (5kms) to Thornton Bridge (Landranger 99 432715). Once over the bridge, turn south along a road which runs through Brafferton and Helperby. Continue through Flawith and Tollerton to join the A19 southbound to York.

Rupert would now have been within The Royal Forest of Galtres, which now exists only as a redundant geographical expression, with place names such as Sutton-on-the-Forest (OS Landranger 100 5864) and Stockton-on-the-Forest (OS Explorer 290 6556) serving to remind us of its former glory. Galtres was originally opened up by the Romans and, by the time of the Civil War, following centuries of exploitation and abuse, there was little timber left. Like many another forest, Galtres had suffered as a result of Henry VIII's programme of naval expansion, which demanded vast amounts of quality timber. The ongoing process of enclosure of land further reduced the woodland cover, transforming it into a decaying bog. Neither Rupert nor any other traveller would have needed the light from York's All Saints to guide him to the city.

To complete the tour, continue through Shipton (OS Explorer 290 5558) and on to Skelton (OS Explorer 290 5756) York, where Rupert's army camped for part of the night of 1 July. By 4.00 am the next day, his army had crossed the Ure at Poppleton. It is worth bearing in mind that Rupert had been on the move since mid-May, had fought a number of engagements and now, with what must have been a footsore army, was about to force a major battle.

Instead of proceeding directly to York as expected, Rupert crossed the River Ure at Boroughbridge, to approach the city from the north.

Appendix I

PHENOMENA

No sooner had the dust settled on the battlefield than stories concerning unexplained phenomena began to circulate locally. There were tales of the battle being fought over and over again by spectral armies in the sky – based, no doubt, upon a well documented incident after Edgehill in 1642. Even so, Marston Moor gradually acquired the reputation of being a troubled place. As late as the nineteenth century, Moor Lane was thought to be haunted by headless horsemen and, according to Leadman, 'the country people could not be induced to traverse it after dark.' Ghostly sightings have continued down to modern times. In November 1932, for example, two motorists saw a small group of ragged men dressed as Cavaliers stagger across the road and into the path of a passing bus which seemed to drive straight through them. In 1968 and again in 1973, there were sightings of men in tattered seventeenth century dress, foundering in the ditch that had separated the armies. Cromwell's ghost has been sighted at Long Marston Hall where, it is claimed, he spent the night before the battle.

Belief in magic and the supernatural is perhaps more in keeping with the seventeenth as opposed to the twenty-first century. The growth in power of the Puritans in the 1640s was certainly accompanied by an increase in the number of prosecutions for witchcraft. The years 1644-47 witnessed the self-styled 'Witchfinder-General', Matthew Hopkins attain the height of his power. A Roundhead pamphlet of 1645 entitled 'Signs and Wonders From Heaven' referred to Hopkins' sterling work in Norfolk where there were

> '40 witches arraigned for their lives, and 20 executed: and that they have done very much harme in that country, and have prophesied of the downfall of the King and his army, and that Prince Rupert shall be no longer shot-free...'

The Roundhead propaganda machine made much of Rupert's dog, 'Boye'. While fighting on the Continent, Rupert had been captured at the Battle of Lemgo in 1638 and held as a prisoner of war in Lintz for three years. During that time, the British Ambassador to Vienna, Lord Arundell, made him a gift of the dog,

One of the casualties of Marston Moor was Rupert's pet poodle, 'Boye'. In this contemporary illustration, Boye is despatched by a musketeer supposedly skilled in 'necromancy'.

a white poodle. The Prince and his pet became very close. As one pamphleteer remarked: 'Then they lye perpetually, in one bed, sometimes the Prince upon the Dogg, and sometimes the Dogg upon the Prince; and what this may in time produce, none but the close Committee can tell'. Boye, according to the Roundheads, was Rupert's 'familiar' – a demon taking the form of an animal assigned to protect a witch. Boye could become invisible at will and was observed protecting Rupert by catching bullets intended for him in its mouth. It was no dog,

> '...but a Witch, a Sorceress, an Enemy to Parliament, a...
> Malignant Cavalier-Dog, that has something of the Devil in or
> about him.'

One of the more usual guises for a witch's 'familiar' was that of a hare. During his captivity in Lintz, Rupert had also tamed a hare, which became as close to him as Boye. Had this been generally known, the pamphleteers would have enjoyed a field-day. Sadly, Boye was one of the casualties at Marston Moor. He had been tied up, but slipped his leash to follow his master into battle. It is likely that Boye was trampled to death, but there remains the possibility that he was deliberately despatched by pike or musket –

Belief in witchcraft was widespread in Stuart England. Matthew Hopkins, the celebrated 'Witchfinder-General' conducted his infamous witch hunts in the years immediately after the English Civil War.

according to Roundhead accounts, by a soldier who happened to be skilled in the art of necromancy. Writing with as much reference to Rupert as to Boye, a Parliamentarian wit remarked:

'Lament poor Cavaliers, ay, howl and yelp
For the great losse of your Malignant Whelp'

Among Boye's talents was the ability to make prophecies 'as well as... Mother Shipton.' This famous seer had prophesied that there would be fought a great battle on Bramham Moor. On 27 May 1644, Bramham Hall was stormed by the Scots, but this could hardly be classed as 'a great battle'. It was more appropriate, therefore, to argue that Long Marston, over four miles from Bramham, was sufficiently close for a match.

Both sides had their soothsayers. Even here, the Roundheads had the better deal, for they had been lucky enough to secure the services of the fashionable astrologer, William Lilley, once a favourite of the King. Such was his influence that he was allegedly offered £50 a year to change sides. The Cavaliers enjoyed the support of Lilley's great rival, George Wharton, a blacksmith's son, who had taken up arms in the opening months of the war. Ultimately, Parliament rewarded Lilley with an annual pension of £100 and punished Wharton by confining him in Newgate.

In August 1644, Lilley produced a pamphlet entitled 'A Prophesy of the White King'. According to an ancient Welsh prophecy, Lilley explained, a battle would take place 'at an ancient seate near a running River... assaulted before and behind, or on all sides... the White & noble King (Charles) shall dye.' Although the Battle of Marston Moor occurred while the pamphlet was still at the printer's, the prophecy was accepted by many as an accurate prediction of the battle and its outcome. Of course, there was no river involved, Charles had not been present and he was not killed, but such minor details were not allowed to obscure the big picture.

Such popular beliefs and superstitions as might be used against the Cavaliers could very easily be turned against their accusers. Some folk, for example, thought that Cromwell was the Devil himself. At the very least, he was alleged to have created a seven year pact with Satan in a bizarre meeting in a wood, witnessed by the Earl of Lindsay. The meeting happened before the Battle of Worcester which took place on 3 September 1651 and which Cromwell won. From that time until his death on 3 September 1658, he prospered. On the day he died, the country was racked by fierce storms while, at Brampton Bryan Castle, near Hereford, Satan was observed dragging a reticent Cromwell through the grounds, apparently en route to Hell, in accordance with their agreement.

A more corporeal, though no less ghoulish, phenomenon concerns the presence of sightseers at Marston Moor – civilians who viewed the battle as a spectator sport. Leadman relates the story of a group of schoolboys who rode out from York to Marston Moor 'just to see the battle'. Among them was a sixteen year old, Christopher Wandesford, whose mother sent another son, George, to fetch him back. Both reached home safely, 'preserved, blessed by God, and not murdered.' Similarly, a Poppleton man, William Prince, apparently watched the battle from the branches of an oak tree until a cannon ball struck his perch. The majority of the audience, however, appears to have been gathered on the high ground to the rear of the Roundhead positions, to be swept away with the fleeing Scots, their curiosity satiated.

Appendix II

EPILOGUE

In the long term, all but one of the participants in the Battle of Marston Moor faded into obscurity. Each had strutted and fretted his hour upon the stage and then was heard no more. Even contemporary stars of the first magnitude such as Sir Thomas Fairfax and Prince Rupert are now forgotten by all but historians and students of the English Civil War.

At Naseby, the final major battle of the war, Rupert led a charge which swept the opposition horse from the field. However, by the time his cavalry had regrouped, the battle – and the war – had been lost. His capitulation at Bristol in September 1645, was the final nail in the coffin. The King was furious, informing his nephew that his:

> *'surrendering it as you did is of so much affliction to me, that it makes me forget not only the consideration of that place, but is likewise the greatest trial of my constancy that hath yet befallen me.'*

Rupert was relieved of his command. At a court-martial, convened at his own request, he was largely cleared of any wrongdoing. When Oxford was finally surrendered to Sir Thomas Fairfax on 20 June 1645, Rupert was permitted to leave the country, sailing for Holland on 5 July. Like many others, he returned to England at the Restoration, to receive an annual allowance of £4,000. In 1668, he was appointed Governor and Constable of Windsor Castle, and became a familiar figure in the Berkshire countryside. He died in 1682.

Sir Thomas Fairfax fought at Naseby as General of Parliament's New Model

Sir Thomas Fairfax

Army and took Rupert's surrender at Bristol. In 1648, when Cavalier unrest flared up into open rebellion, Fairfax presided at the siege of Colchester. The garrison surrendered on 26 August and many of the defenders were transported to the West Indies. Two of the leaders, Sir George Lisle and Sir Charles Lucas, a veteran of Marston Moor, were shot on Fairfax's orders, suggesting that he was not so high minded as to rise above the temptation to settle old scores. Disassociating himself from the trial and execution of the King, he resigned his commission eighteen months later, retiring at the age of thirty-eight to the Yorkshire estates which he had inherited upon the death of his father, Ferdinando. He employed the poet, Andrew Marvell, as a tutor for his daughter, and wrote some indifferent verse himself. Crippled by gout, 'The Rider of the White Horse' spent his final years confined to a wheelchair. He died in 1671.

The Marquis of Newcastle, whose first wife had died shortly after the Battle of Seacroft Moor, married again in exile. His new bride, Margaret Lucas, was the sister of Sir Charles Lucas and thirty years Newcastle's junior. They rented a house in Antwerp which had belonged to Reubens the artist. After the Restoration, a Parliamentary bill was introduced on Newcastle's behalf, aimed at restoring 'all his Honours, Manors, Lands and Tenements in England, whereof he was in possession on 23 October 1642'. His wife reckoned that his allegiance to the Crown had cost him £1,000,000, and he spent the rest of his life working to repair his

fortunes. He died on Christmas Day 1676, aged 83.

The minor players on the losing side were not all so lucky. Sir Henry Slingsby, the Yorkshire diarist, had his estates sequestered, yet always stood ready to participate in plans for rebellion. On 25 May 1658, he was brought to trial on a charge of high

The diary of the Yorkshire Cavalier, Sir Henry Slingsby, is a valuable source for historians, although it is actually more of a memoir, entries covering key periods having been made retrospectively.

treason – specifically:

> *'That he did traitorously advisedly and maliciously combine together and plot to betray and yield up the... Garrison of Hull unto Charles Stuart.'*

In fact, Slingsby may have been encouraged and betrayed by a double-agent in the employ of Cromwell, who was keen to make an example of him. After a show trial, during which he was allowed no counsel, Slingsby was condemned to death and beheaded on Tower Hill on 8 June 1658. According to one report, he enjoyed the distinction of being the last person to have his head exhibited on Micklegate Bar in York.

Similarly unfortunate was the Earl of Derby, who was held responsible for Rupert's bloody assault on Bolton. Like Slingsby, he remained a committed Royalist, participating in the Worcester campaign in 1651. Having raised a force of Lancashire Cavaliers, he marched south, only to be stopped at Wigan by Roundhead Colonel Robert Lilburne. Wounded in the mouth, he eventually reached Worcester with only thirty men. After the Battle of Worcester, which took place on 3 September, he fled back to Cheshire, where he was captured. Removed to Bolton, he was beheaded on a scaffold erected in the market place, 'with every circumstance of rudeness and barbarity.' His estates on the Isle of Man were handed over to Fairfax but, to his credit, Sir Thomas ensured that Derby's widow continued to receive the ordinary rents.

The would-be turncoats, Sir John Hotham and son, did not survive the war. They were executed on 2 January and 1 January 1645 respectively. Among Newcastle's belongings, abandoned after Marston Moor, had been found letters which proved – to Parliament's satisfaction – their intention 'to betray Hull to the enemy.' Arch-turncoat, Sir John Urry, ultimately joined the Marquis of Montrose, with whom he shared defeat at the Battle of Carbisdale. Wounded and captured, he was executed on 29 May 1650.

Of Urry's fellow Scots, David Leslie went on to defeat Montrose at Philiphaugh on 13 September 1645 and to be defeated himself by Cromwell at Dunbar on 3 September 1650. A year later, he fought for Charles II at Worcester, where he was taken prisoner. He remained in captivity until the Restoration after which, as Lord Newark, he retired into private life. The Earl of Leven was nominally in command of the army which Leslie – his nephew – led at Dunbar. As such, he, too, was taken prisoner and

In 1657, Oliver Cromwell, who was already addressed as 'Highness', was offered the crown, a situation he would have accepted but for the opposition of the Army.

John Lambert was one of Cromwell's closest collaborators on the field of battle. He was a veteran of many encounters, including Marston Moor, and engineered Cromwell's victories at Preston, Dunbar and Worcester - although his boss took the credit. In 1657, Cromwell expressed the extent of his gratitude by sacking him.

confined to the Tower of London, until released on his own surety of £20,000.

The man who gained most from Marston Moor was Oliver Cromwell. Before the battle, during the interrogation of a Roundhead prisoner, it is said that Prince Rupert eagerly posed the question: 'Is Cromwell there?' This is unlikely as, at that time, Cromwell's reputation was not of such magnitude as to commend itself to the Prince's attention. His reputation as a soldier was largely determined by his appointment as Lord Protector. Thus, in retrospect, would he become the victor of Winceby – where his horse had been killed and Sir Thomas Fairfax had saved the day. At Marston Moor, it would be argued, he had been solely responsible for breaking Byron's cavalry. And he alone had

In 1650, Sir Thomas Fairfax retired to his favourite residence, Nun Appleton, to live the life of a country gentleman, employing the poet, Andrew Marvell, as a tutor for his daughter.

In 1659, Marvell became MP for Hull. His statue stands near the market place in the city, not far from Beverley Gate.

triumphed at Dunbar – a success he owed to a strategy engineered by Major-General John Lambert. Failures, such as the Second Battle of Newbury, where Lord Goring's Cavaliers put Cromwell's cavalry to flight, were conveniently forgotten. The first article of Parliament's 'Humble Petition and Advice' of 25 May 1657, addressed to Cromwell, speaks volumes:

That your Highness will be pleased by and under the name and style of Lord Protector of the Commonwealth of England, Scotland and Ireland, and the dominions and territories thereunto belonging, to hold and exercise the office of Chief Magistrate of these nations, and to govern according to this petition and advice in all things therein contained, and in all other things according to the laws of these nations, and not otherwise: that your Highness will be pleased during your lifetime to appoint and declare the person who shall, immediately after your death, succeed you in the Government of these nations.'

As with many a dictator, however, Cromwell in death was treated with far less respect than Cromwell in life. When he died in 1658, his body was interred in Westminster Abbey with as much pomp and circumstance as would attend the burial of any monarch. Even so, the diarist, John Evelyn reported that it was 'the joyfullest funeral that I ever saw; for there was none that cried but dogs, which the soldiers hooted away with a barbarous noise, drinking and taking tobacco in the streets as they went.' In 1661, Charles II – 'the Merry Monarch' – had the decaying corpse removed, hanged at Tyburn and decapitated, the head subsequently becoming a collector's item.

In the longer term, too, history has been less than kind to Cromwell. His depredations in Ireland at Drogheda and Wexford can no longer be easily dismissed by his apologists as 'accidental' or 'acceptable by the standards of the time.' In a recent (2002) television poll to find the top ten Britons of all time, Cromwell stumbled in last, with only 2.8 per cent of the vote, lagging well behind such luminaries as John Lennon and Diana, Princess of Wales. He would not have been amused.

Appendix III

ARMS AND ATTIRE

In 1470, Edward IV had quelled a rebellion in Lincolnshire led by Sir Robert Welles. At the Battle of Empingham, to the north of Stamford, the rebels fled, discarding their jackets and emblems which identified them as rebels – thus giving the encounter its alternative title: The Battle of Lose-coat Field. Two centuries later, at Marston Moor, the action of Sir Thomas Fairfax in discarding his white 'signal' at Marston Moor, probably saved his life. It seems surprising, in itself, that no one recognised 'The Rider of the White Horse', one of the most charismatic figures of the war. By throwing away his emblem, however, Sir Thomas was able to retreat into the anonymity of the enemy's ranks.

The very fact that the Roundheads needed such a token in order to distinguish them from the Cavaliers does serve as a reminder that there was no standard 'blue and grey' to distinguish the combatants, and throughout the war, there were many instances of casualties sustained by friendly fire. Rupert's troops at Marston Moor, consisting in large part of 'private' armies, presented something of a multi-coloured spectacle, with Newcastle's 'Whitcoats', Tillier's 'Greencoats', Rupert's own 'Bluecoats' and so on. Similarly, while red figured strongly in the tunics of Manchester's Army of the Eastern Association, there was little uniformity in the Roundheads' attire.

Some of the arms in use were quite primitive. Thus, one of the casualties of Marston Moor, the Cavalier, Colonel Charles Slingsby, is recorded as having been killed by the blow of a battle axe. Similarly, excavations at Wakefield's Sandal Castle uncovered arrow heads, believed to have been ready for use during the siege of 1645, while the 'clubmen' of the West Riding towns would make do, as Fairfax pointed out, 'with clubs and such rustic weapons.'

In 1642, the Earl of Essex was planning to make use of archers, even though the archer's heir, the musketeer, was coming of age, and capable of inflicting considerable damage. The main problem for a musketeer was his weapon's weight, which made the use of a rest necessary. Elton, writing in *The Complete Body of the Art Military*, quotes musketeers' criticisms:

'...our Rests are of little or no use unto us in time of

139

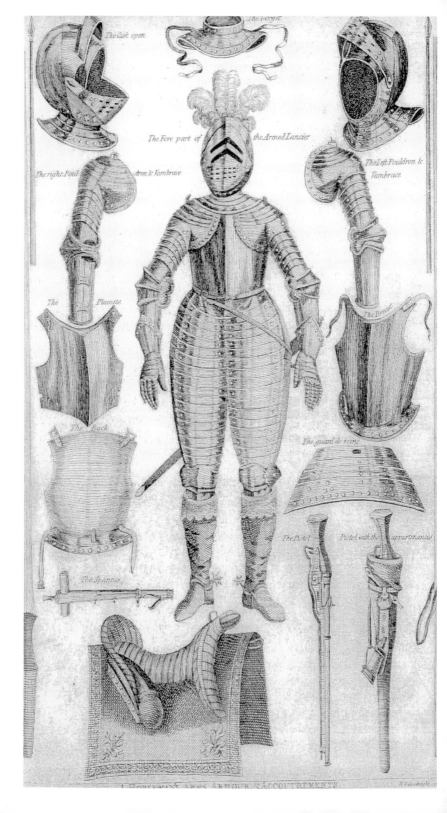

The Cask open

The Gorget

The Fore part of the Armed Lancier

The right Pouldron, Avon, & Vambrace

The Left Pouldron & Vambrace

The Placatte

The Breast

The Back

The guard de reine

The Spanner

The Pistol

Pistol with the appurtenances

A HORSEMANS ARMS ARMOUR & ACCOUTRIMENTS

skirmishing, fit they are, we confesse, in the Military Gardens,
but in time of battail both troublesome and cumbersome unto
us.'

The majority of musketeers were armed with the matchlock, reasonably accurate at up to 100 yards or so. Once the contraption had been erected, a charge of powder would be placed in the barrel, followed by a ball, accompanied by wadding. A measure of gunpowder would then be emptied into a pan, and a lighted taper pressed into a metal trigger mechanism. When the musket was fired, the taper would ignite the powder in the pan, causing a flame to enter the barrel and discharge the ball. An experienced musketeer would be able to fire three shots per minute.

The musketeer was also challenging the pikeman as the mainstay of the infantry. Two-thirds of Leven's army at Marston Moor consisted of musketeers, although the pike still had an important role to play. The length of a pike varied between sixteen and eighteen feet, although some were shorter. All pikeman, advised Markham in *The Souldier's Accidence,*

'...shall have good combe-caps for their heads, well lined
with quilted caps, curaces for their bodies of nimble and good
mould, being high pike proof; large and well compact gordgetts
for their neckes, fayr and close joined taches, to arm to mid-
thigh; as for the pouldron or the vantbrace, they may be spared,
because they are cumbersome. All this armour is to be rather
of russet, sanguine, or blacke colour, than white or milled, for
it will keep the longer from rust.'

Warming to his theme, Markham continues:

'These shall have strong, straight, yet nimble pikes of
ashwood, well headed with steel, and armed with plates
downward from the head, at least four foote, and the full size
or length of every pike shalbe fifteene foote besides the head...
These pikemen shall also have good, sharpe, and broade
swords (of which Turkie and Bilboe are best), strong
scabbards, chapt with iron, girdle, hangars or bautricke of
strong leather; and lastly, if to the pikeman's head peece be

Full body armour, although occasionally donned
at the beginning of the war, soon fell out of favour.
One exception involved the Roundhead, Sir Arthur
Haselrige's, Cuirassiers or 'Lobsters as they were
popularly known. The king once remarked that if
Haselrige was as well victualled as fortified, he
might endure a siege of seven years.

fastened a small ring of iron, and to the right side of his back peece (below his girdle) an iron hooke, to hang his steele cap upon, it will be a great ease to the souldier, and a nimble carriage in the time of long marches.'

Theory, of course, was often a far cry from reality; after Marston Moor, the armies of both sides were threadbare.

As the war progressed, one shortage which became particularly acute was that of horses. At the beginning of the war, it was the King who could command the better horses and the horsemen, veterans of the hunting field, to accompany them. The cavalryman, according to General George Monck, should wear:

'An Head-piece with three small iron Bars to defend the Face, Back, and Breast; all three Pistol proof: a Gauntlet for his left hand, or a good long Buff Glove. A Girdle of double Buff about eight inches broad, which is to be worn under the skirts of his Doublet, and to be hooked unto his Doublet, and made so that it may be fastened together before...'

In addition to his sword, he carried a brace of pistols.

Mounts of poorer quality generally found their way to the dragoons, or mounted infantrymen. According to Markham, these:

'footmen on horesbacke... are of singular use in all actions of warre; their armes defensive, are an open head-piece with cheeks, and a good buffe coat, with deep skirts; and for offensive armes, they have a fair dragon, fitted with an iron worke to be caryed in a belt of leather, which is buckled over the right shoulder, and under the left arme, having a turnill of iron with a ring, through which the piece runnes up and downe...'

As Firth has stated, however, the term 'dragoon' was applied to a mounted infantryman carrying any kind of musket or firelock.

Artillery played a relatively small part in the pitched battles of the Civil War. Its main function lay in siege operations. Thus, while heavy guns were employed in the Siege of York, there was only a limited role for them at Marston Moor, and the effort expended in dragging them the length and breadth of the county was often barely repaid in terms of their utility.

Appendix IV

SOURCES

~ I ~

Contemporary accounts of Civil War battles are not models of accuracy, although the partisanship they display is often of interest in itself. The first account given here is provided by the diary of Sir Henry Slingsby. Although Slingsby's own regiment remained in York, Slingsby may have participated in the battle as a gentleman volunteer. The second account is taken from *A More Exact Relation Of the Late Battle Near York* by Leonard Watson, 'Scoutmaster-General' in the Earl of Manchester's army, whose function, in the words of Firth, was 'to send out scouts, and to reconnoitre the ground round the place where the army was encamped and the country through which it was to march.'

A Cavalier's Account (Sir Henry Slingsby):

The prince [Rupert] was now come within 3 or 4 miles of York upon the forest side and sent in to my Lord of Newcastle to meet him with those forces he had in York; and it was upon 2 July 1644 when my Lord marched out with all those forces he had, leaving only in the town Colonel Bellasyse's Regiment, Sir Thomas Glemham's Regiment and my own, which was the City Regiment. The prince passed over at Poppleton where the Scots had made a bridge of boats and followed the Scots in the rear, who were now upon their march towards Marston, and in so much haste as if they meant to march clear away; the prince followed on and made a halt at Marston town, the Scots there marching up the field, the direct way to Tadcaster; but upon the top of the hill, they faced... towards the prince, who till now was persuaded that they meant not to give him battle, but to march quite away. Now the prince bestired himself, putting his men in such order as he intended to fight and sending away to my Lord Newcastle to march with all speed. The enemy made some shot at him as they were drawing up into Battalia and the first shot killed a son of Sir

Gilbert Haughton, who was a captain in the prince's army, but this was only showing their teeth, for after 4 shots made them give over, and in Marston corn fields fell to singing psalms: the prince's horse had the right wing, my Lord Goring the left; the foot disposed of with most advantage to fight, some of them drawn off to line the hedges of the cornfields where the enemy must come to charge. The enemy's forces consisting of 3 parts, the Scots, Manchester and Fairfax, were one mixed with another; Cromwell having the left wing drawn into 5 bodies of horse, came off the Cony Warren, by Bilton bream, to charge our horse, and upon their first charge routed them; they flew along by Wilstrop woodside, as fast and as thick could be; yet our left Wing pressed as hard upon their right wing, and pursued them over the Hill; after our horse was gone they fell upon our foot, and although a great while they maintained the fight yet at last they were cut down and most part either taken or killed. Here I lost a nephew, Colonel John Fenwick and a kinsman, Sir Charles Slingsby, both of them slain in the field; the former could not be found to have his body brought off, the latter was found and buried in York Minster. They pursued not, but kept the field as many as were left, for they fled as fast as we and their 3 Generals gone, thinking all had been lost. We came late to York, we made a great confusion; for at the bar [Micklegate] none was suffered to come in but such as were of the town, so that the whole street was thronged up to the bar with wounded and lame people, who made a pitiful cry among them.

A Roundhead's Account
(Scoutmaster-General Leonard Watson):

The enemy, thinking we dislodged because we would avoid fighting, and being resolved to fight with us, they drew out five thousand Horse and Dragoons, the vanguard of their army, and with them took the Moor near Marston, about nine of the clock on Tuesday, and came up close to the rear of our carriages.

We feeling that they were in earnest to fight, and we as much as they desiring it, presently commanded all our foot and ordnance to come back with all speed, the vanguard of which was gone some five miles towards Cawood, and was with much difficulty to be brought back. The enemy in the meanwhile, drawing up with part of their foot close to our noses, so near that we had not liberty to take the Moor, and to put ourselves into battalia, so that we were put to drawn our men into a cornfield close to the Moor, making way by our pioneers to get ground to extend the wings of our army to such a distance, that we might conveniently fight; which was very difficult for us to attain. The right wing of our army being placed just by Marston Town side, the town on our right hand, fronting on the East, and as our foot and horse came up, we formed our battalia and the left wing, still desiring to gain as much of the left point as we could, so that at last we came with the utmost point of our left wing to Tockwith; being a mile and a half in length; the enemy being drawn up just under us, the wings of their army extending a little further than ours in length, but the hedges and our dragoons secured the flanks. About two of the clock, the great ordnance of both sides began to play, but with small success to either; about five of the clock we had a general silence on both sides, each expecting who should begin the charge, there being a small ditch and a bank betwixt us and the Moor, through which we must pass if we would charge them upon the Moor, or they pass it, if they would charge us in the great cornfield and closes; so that it was a great disadvantage to him that would begin the charge, feeling the ditch must somewhat disturb their order, and the other would be ready in good ground and order, to charge them before they could recover it.

In this posture we stood till seven of the clock, so that it was concluded on our sides, that there would be no engagement that night, neither of the two armies agreeing to begin the charge: And surely had two such armies (drawn up so close one to the other, being of both wings within musket shot), departed without fighting, I think it would have been as great a wonder as has been seen in England. the enemy had in the Field in all, some fourteen thousand Foot, and nine thousand Horse, and some twenty five pieces of ordnance. The right wing of their Horse was commanded by Prince Rupert, who had it in some twelve divisions of

*Horse, consisting of one hundred troops, and might be five
thousand men. The left wing of their Horse was
commanded by Urry, with all the remainder of their Horse.
The right wing of our Horse was commanded by Sir Thomas
Fairfax, consisting of 80 troops, being his own and the
Scotch Horse. The left wing of our Horse was commanded by
Lieutenant General Cromwell, with all his own Horse, and
the Earl of Manchester's, and some of the Scotch Horse,
being in all about 70 troops. Our Foot being twenty eight
regiments, were disposed into twelve brigades. About half an
hour after seven o'clock at night, we seeing the enemy would
not charge us, we resolved by the help of God, to charge
them, and so the sign being given, we marched down to the
charge. In which you might have seen the bravest fight in the
world; Two such disciplined armies marching to a charge.
We came down the hill in the bravest order, and with the
greatest resolution that was ever seen: I mean the left wing
of our Horse led by Cromwell, which was to charge their
right wing led by Rupert, in which was all their gallant men:
they being resolved, if they could scatter Cromwell, all were
their own.*

*All the Earl of Manchester's Foot being three Brigades,
began the charge with their bodies against the Marquess of
Newcastle and Prince Rupert's bravest Foot. In a moment
we were passed the ditch into the Moor, upon equal grounds
with the enemy, our men going in a running march. Our
front divisions of Horse charged their front, Lieutenant
General Cromwell's division of three hundred Horse, in
which himself was in person, charged the first division of
Prince Rupert's, in which himself was in person. The rest of
ours charged other divisions of theirs, but with such
admirable valour, as it was to the astonishment of all the old
soldiers of the army. Cromwell's own division had a hard
pull of it: for they were charged by Rupert's bravest men in
both front and flank: they stood at the sword's point a pretty
while, hacking one another: but at last (it so pleased God)
he broke through them, scattering them before him like a
little dust.*

*At the same instant the rest of our horse of that wing, had
wholly broken all Prince Rupert's horse on their right wing,
and were in the chase of them beyond their left wing: our*

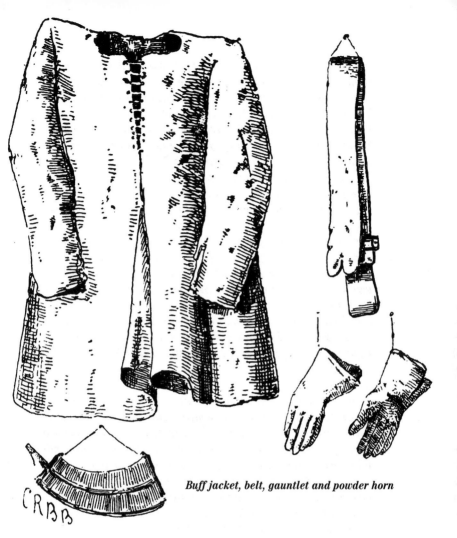

Buff jacket, belt, gauntlet and powder horn

Foot on the right hand of us (being only the Earl of Manchester's Foot) went on by our side dispersing the enemy's Foot almost as fast as they charged them, still going by our side, cutting them down that we carried the whole Field before us, thinking the victory wholly ours, and nothing to be done but to kill and take prisoners; not knowing that the enemy's left wing, led by Urry, had done as much to our right (led by Sir Thomas Fairfax), they wholly carrying the Field before them, utterly routing all our Horse and Foot, so that there was not a man left standing before them, most of the Horse and Foot of that wing, and our main battell, retreating in haste towards

Tadcaster and Cawood, thinking the day lost, as the enemy's right wing did towards York. The enemy being in pursuit and chase of retreating men, followed them to our carriages, but had slain few of them: for indeed they ran away before the enemy charged them. Just then came our Horse and Foot from the chase of their right wing, and seeing the business not well in our right, came in a very good order to a second charge with all the enemy's Horse and Foot that had disordered our right wing and main battell. And here came the business of the day (nay almost of the Kingdom) to be disputed upon this second charge.

The enemy seeing us to come in such a gallant posture to charge them, left all thoughts of pursuit, and began to think that they must fight again for that victory which they thought they had already got. They marching down the hill upon us, from our carriages, so that they fought upon the same ground, and with the same front that our right wing had before stood to receive their charge; and we stood in the same ground, and with the same front which they had when they began the charge.

Our three brigades of Foot of the Earl of Manchester's being on our right hand, on we went with great resolution, charging them so home, one while their Horse, and then again their Foot, and our Foot and Horse seconding each other with such valour, made them fly before us, that it was hard to say which did the better our Horse or Foot. Major General Leslie seeing us thus pluck a victory out of the enemy's hands, professed Europe had no better soldiers.

Many of the surviving letters written soon after the encounter are semi-official documents, intended primarily to convey news of the outcome. Sir William Fairfax, cousin to Sir Thomas, managed to scribble the following brief personal note to his wife, to let her know he was safe. Historians have described the letter as disappointing, in view of the paucity of detail concerning the battle. To the recipient, Lady Frances, it must have been priceless. In September 1644, Sir William was killed in an action to secure Montgomery Castle.

For my dear wife the Lady Frances Fairfax at her house near Charing Cross.

My Dear Heart - I know when you hear of our great battle with Prince Rupert you will be very fearful for me; therefore I write to satisfy thee that God has also, at this time, preserved me from any hurt at all. We have beaten Prince Rupert to some tune, and routed all his army and taken his ordnance. We have killed above a thousand of his men, but what prisoners I know not yet, but there is very many. The battle was fought in Marston Fields, not far from Quinton Ludstone's house, the hour at five o'clock in the afternoon. I cannot stay the messenger, so that you must excuse me to all my friends, and tell them I had not any paper but this, and it was a piece of a letter. Sir Thomas Fairfax is wounded in the face, but not much worse. Colonel Lambert is very well, but most of his officers killed and hurt. My service to my Lady Sheffield, and my wife, Lambert, and all the rest of my friends. Tom Smith is slain, so I rest thy dear husband.

Will Fairfax

~ III ~

The following affidavit of Richard Easby is testimony to the location of the gate at which a young servant was killed while trying to assist fleeing Cavalier horse. Such tales are often dismissed - rather unfairly - as 'the extravagances of 19th century antiquarians'.

I, Richard Easby, of Upper Poppleton, in the Ainstey of the City of York, farmer, do declare that I am now at the age of sixty-one years and upwards, and am the son of Richard Easby, late of Wilstrop in the same County, farmer, that I have seen the painting in the possession of Mr John Daniel of Holgate Lane, in the suburbs of the City of York, gentleman, which is a faithful representation of the Old Cottage at Wilstrop, which upwards of four hundred years ago was in the occupation of my ancestors, and so continued until about one hundred years ago, when a new farmhouse at present occupied by John Firby was erected about two hundred yards off the Old Cottage, and to the south of the said old Cottage; and which new farm-house was occupied by my family until Lady Day, eighteen hundred and seventy-seven, when my brother George Easby, who was up to his death tenant of the new farm-house, died there. That I have understood from and had told me by my late father and grandfather, who themselves had had the same handed down to them from father to son, that a general of cavalry of the Parliamentary army slept in the said Old Cottage on the night preceding the Battle of Marston Moor. And also that there was a gateway about four hundred yards south of the said Old Cottage, and near to the north-east corner of Wilstrop Wood, being about twenty yards east of an old thatched cottage long in the occupation of William Hudson, gamekeeper, and known locally by the name of the gamekeeper's house, and which gateway would then lead from the old inclosure on to the Moor, and then, and at present from the bridge over the ditch, which is the boundary between the townships of Wilstrop and Moor Monkton. A servant girl ran out from the back door of the gamekeeper's house to open the gate in the said gateway for some troopers forming, it is

A representation (reproduced from Leadman's **Battles Fought in Yorkshire***) of the cottage from which the servant girl ran to open a gate for the fleeing Cavaliers.*

believed, according to the best authorities, a portion of the right wing of Rupert's cavalry flying from the cavalry of the left wing of the Parliamentary Army, the said servant girl, in the head-long haste of the troopers, being run over and there killed. In witness whereof I have hereunto set my hand this sixth day of August, eighteen hundred and seventy-nine.

Richard Easby.

~ **IV** ~

The initial commission of the Earl of Newcastle comprised 'the preservation of this town [Newcastle], the County of Northumberland, and the Bishoprick of Durham'. The following extract is from the Earl's 'Declaration', in which he attempted to justify his march into Yorkshire. At the time of writing, the prospect of intervention by the Scots was not yet visible on the horizon.

'But it has not pleased God that our neighbours in Yorkshire and the adjacent Counties should enjoy the like calm which hath moved many of the prime Noblemen and Gentlemen of the County of York to remonstrate unto me their sufferings, which they endure from Sir John Hotham, his son, and many their seditious and outrageous Complices, and so desire my aid for the redressing of them, and repressing their tumultuous oppressions, before they shall swell to that height, as it cannot stand with the safety of the Persons and Estates of his Majesty's good subjects in Yorkshire, to make any expressions of their loyalty and allegiance to His Majesty, unless by some of my forces they be speedily comforted and relieved.

I having seriously weighted the purport of my Commission, and finding it not only consistent with, and agreeable to the same; but knowing well His Majesty's sacred intention and constant resolution to secure the lives and liberties of his subjects by all means which he can compass: I have now resolved to assist his Majesty's distressed subjects in the County of York with competent forces; and yet to leave this town [Newcastle] so strongly guarded, that their former security shall be no way discontinued or intercepted.'

The Solemn League and Covenant was ratified by the Scottish General Assembly on 17 August 1643. From this date, one may argue, the fate of Charles I was sealed. The Covenant consisted of six articles. From the point of view of the Scots, Article I, establishing the supremacy of the Church of Scotland, was the most significant. As far as the English Parliament was concerned, Article VI, in which the Scots committed themselves to armed intervention in the Civil War, was the only one that mattered. Loyalty to the king is stressed throughout.

I. That we shall sincerely, really and constantly, through the grace of God, endeavour, in our several places and callings, the preservation of the reformed religion in the Church of Scotland, in doctrine, worship, discipline, and government, against our common enemies; the reformation of religion in the kingdoms of England and Ireland, in doctrine, worship, discipline, and government, according to the Word of God, and the example of the best reformed Churches; and shall endeavour to bring the Churches of God in the three kingdoms to the nearest conjunction and uniformity in religion, Confession of Faith, Form of Church Government, Directory for Worship and Catechising; that we, and our posterity after us, may, as brethren, live in faith and love, and the Lord may delight to dwell in the midst of us.

II. That we shall, in like manner, without respect of persons, endeavour the extirpation of Popery, Prelacy (that is, Church government by archbishops, bishops, their chancellors and commissioners, deans, deans and chapters, archdeacons, and all other ecclesiastical officers depending on that hierarchy), superstition, heresy, schism, profaneness, and whatsoever shall be found contrary to sound doctrine and the power of Godliness; lest we partake in other men's sins, and thereby be in danger to receive of their plagues; and that the Lord may be one, and His name one, in the three kingdoms.

III. We shall, with the same sincerity, reality, and constancy, in our several vocations, endeavour, with our estates and lives, mutually to preserve the rights and privileges of the Parliaments, and the liberties of the kingdoms; and to preserve and defend theKing's Majesty's person and authority, in the preservation and defence of the true religion and liberties of the kingdoms; that the world may bear witness with our consciences of our loyalty, and that we have no other thoughts or intentions to diminish His Majesty's just power and greatness.

IV. We shall also, with all faithfulness, endeavour the discovery of all such as have been or shall be incendiaries, malignants, or evil instruments, be hindering the reformation of religion, dividing the king from his people, or one on the kingdoms from another, or making any faction or parties among the people, contrary to this League and Covenant; that they may be brought to public trial, and receive condign punishment, as the degree of their offences shall require or deserve, or the supreme judicatories of both kingdoms respectively, or others having power from them for that effect, shall judge convenient.

V. And whereas the happiness of a blessed peace between these kingdoms, denied in former times to our progenitors, is by the good providence of GOD, granted unto us, according to our place and interest, endeavour that they may remain conjoined in a firm peace and union to all posterity; and that justice may be done upon the willful opposers thereof, in manner expressed in the precendent article.

VI. We shall also, according to our places and callings, in this common cause of religion, liberty, and peace of the kingdoms, assist and defend all those that enter into this League and Covenant, in the maintaining and pursuing thereof; and shall not suffer ourselves, directly or indirectly, by whatsoever combination, persuasion, or terror, to be divided or withdrawn from this blessed union and conjunction, whether to make defection to the contrary part, or to give ourselves to a detestable indifferency or neutrality in this cause, which so much concerneth the glory of God, the good of the kingdom, and honour of the King; but shall, all the days of our lives, zealously and constantly continue therein against all opposition, and promote the same, according to our power, against all lets and impediments whatsoever; and what we are not able ourselves to suppress or overcome, we shall reveal and make known, that it may be timely prevented or removed: All which we shall do as in the sight of God.

On 24 November 1644, Parliament proposed terms for peace. One cannot but doubt the sincerity of the offer, for the document with which Charles was presented at Oxford included a lengthy list of those of his supporters 'who shall expect no pardon.' Heading the roll, with the status of Public Enemy Number One was Prince Rupert. Bulstrode Whitlock, one of the Parliamentary commissioners reported that when Rupert and his brother saw the list, 'they fell into a laughter, at which the King seemed displeased, and bid them be quiet.' Some of the nominees, such as Newcastle, were included to enable Parliament to sequester their estates. The victory at Marston Moor had obviously emboldened Parliament in terms of the demands it was prepared to make, and the list included leading Cavaliers who fought there.

That the persons who shall expect no pardon be only these following: Rupert and Maurice, Counts Palatine of the Rhine, James Earl of Derby, John Earl of Bristol, William Earl of Newcastle, Francis Lord Cottington, George Lord Digby, Matthew Wren, Bishop of Ely, Sir Robert Heath, Knt., Dr. Bramhall, Bishop of Derry, Sir William Widdrington, Col. George Goring, Henry Jermyn, Esq., Sir

CRBB

Ralph Hopton, Sir John Byron, Sir Francis Doddington, Sir Francis Strangways, Mr. Endymion Porter, Sir George Radcliffe, Sir Marmaduke Langdale, Henry Vaughan, Esq., now called Sir Henry Vaughan, Sir Francis Windebank, Sir Richard Grenvile, Mr Edward Hyde, now called Sir Edward Hyde, Sir John Marley, Sir Nicholas Cole, Sir Thomas Riddell, junior, Sir John Culpepper, Mr. Richard Lloyd, now called Sir Richard Lloyd, Mr. David Jenkins, Sir George Strode, George Cartaret Esq., now called Sir George Cartaret, Sir Charles Dallison, Knt., Richard Lane, Esq., now called Sir Richard Lane, Sir Edward Nicholas, John Ashburnham, Esq., Sir Edward Herbert, Knt., Attorney-General, Earl of Traquair, Lord Harris, Lord Reay, George Gordon, sometime Marquis of Huntley, James Graham, someone Earl of Montrose, Robert Maxwell, late Earl of Nithsdale, Robert Dalyel, sometime Earl of Carnwath, James Gordon, sometime Viscount of Aboyne, Ludovic Lindsay, sometime Earl of Crawford, James Ogilvy, sometime Lord Ogilvy, Patrick Ruthven, sometime Earl of Forth, James King, sometime Lord Eythin, Alaster MacDonald, Irvine the younger of Drum, Gordon the younger of Gight, Leslie of Auchintoul, Col. John Cochrane, Graham of Gorthie, Mr. John Maxwell, sometime pretended Bishop of Ross, and all such others as being processed by the Estates for treason, shall be condemned before the Act of Oblivion be passed.

Appendix VI

FURTHER READING

Barker, Anthony, *A Battlefield Atlas of the English Civil War,* Ian Allan Ltd., 1986.

Barratt, John, *The Battle for York, Marston Moor 1644,* Tempus, 2002.

Barrett, C. R. B. *Battles And Battlefields in England,* A. D. Innes & Co., 1896.

Bennett, Martyn, *Traveller's Guide to the Battlefields of the English Civil War,* Webb & Bower, 1990.

Burne, Alfred H. *The Battlefields of England,* 1951.

Churchill, Winston, *A History of the English-Speaking Peoples Vol II*, Cassell, 1956.

Clarendon, Edward Hyde, Earl of, *The History of the Rebellion and Civil Wars in England,* OUP, 1843.

Cowan, Edward J *Montrose, For Covenant and King*, Weidenfield & Nicolson, 1977.

Evans, David, *The Battle of Marston Moor,* Stuart Press, 1994.

Fairburn, Neil, *A Traveller's Guide to the Battlefields of Britain,* Evans Brothers, 1983.

Firth, C. H. *Cromwell's Army*, Methuen, 1921.

Firth, C. H. *Marston Moor, Transactions of the Royal Historical Society,* New Series Vol XII, 1898.

Fraser, Antonia, *Cromwell Our Chief of Men*, Mandarin, 1989.

Gardiner, S. R., *A History of the Great Civil War Vol I*, Longman, 1888.

Gardiner, S. R. *The Constitutional Documents of the Puritan Revolution 1625-1660*, Oxford, 1906.

Green, Colonel Howard, *Guide to the Battlefields of Britain and Ireland,* Constable, 1973.

Howes, Audrey and Foreman, Martin *Town and Gun,* Kingston Press, 1999.

Kenyon, John & Ohlmeyer, *The Civil Wars: A Military History of England and Scotland 1638-1660*, OUP, 1998.

Kinross, John, *The Battlefields of Britain*, David & Charles, 1979.

Leadman, A. D. H. *Battles Fought in Yorkshire*, Bradbury, Agnew & Co., 1891.

Morrah, Patrick, *Prince Rupert of the Rhine*, Constable, 1976.

Many writers have been inspired by the Battle of Marston Moor. Among them was Sir Walter Scott, who took Marston Moor as a starting point for his 1813 poem, 'Rokeby'.

Newman, Peter, *The Battle of Marston Moor,* Antony Bird, 1981.
Newman, P. R. *Atlas of the English Civil War,* Croom Helm, 1985.
Parsons, D (ed), *The Diary of Sir Henry Slingsby*, Longman, 1836.
Reid, Stuart, *All the King's Armies*, Spellmount, 1998.
Rogers, Colonel H.C.B., *Battles & Generals of the Civil Wars*, Seeley Service & Co., 1968.

Seymour, William, *Battles in Britain 1642-1746*, Sidgwick & Jackson, 1975.

Smurthwaite, David, *The Complete Guide to the Battlefields of Britain*, Michael Joseph, 1993.

Trease, Geoffrey, *Portrait of a Cavalier: William Cavendish*, First Duke of Newcastle, Macmillan, 1979.

Warner, David, *British Battlefields: The North*, Osprey Publishing, 1972.

Wedgwood, C.V. *The King's War 1641-1647,* Collins, 1958.

Wedgwood, C.V. *Civil War Battlefields 1642-46*, BBC, 1959,

Wenham, Peter, *The Great and Close Siege of York 1644*, The Roundwood Press, 1970.

Wetherell, J.E., *Fields of Fame in England and Scotland*, Macmillan, 1923.

Woolrych, Austin, *Battles of the English Civil War,* B. T. Batsford, 1961.

Young, Brigadier Peter, *Marston Moor 1644: The Campaign and the Battle,* The Roundwood Press, 1970.

Young, Brigadier Peter and Adair John, *From Hastings to Culloden,* The Roundwood Press, 1979.

Young, Brigadier Peter and Emberton, Wilfrid, *Sieges of the Great Civil War,* Bell & Hyman 1978.

Note: Contemporary writings are reproduced in Peter Young's *Marston Moor 1644: The Campaign and the Battle,* as appendix material, and are the sources of a number of the quotations in this book.

Appendix VI

TIMELINE

Civil War Timeline

12 May 1641	Execution of Earl of Strafford.
1 December 1641	Parliament presents Charles I with The Grand Remonstrance.
4 January 1642	Charles I attempts to arrest the Five Members.
10 January 1642	Charles I leaves London.
18 March 1642	Charles I arrives in York.
23 April 1642	Charles I refused entry to Hull.
2-3 July 1642	The Navy declares for Parliament.
22 August 1642	Charles I raises his Standard at Nottingham/First English Civil War begins.
23 September 1642	First battle of Civil War takes place at Powick Bridge, where Prince Rupert defeats Colonel John Brown.
23 October 1642	Armies of Charles I and Earl of Essex meet at Edgehill – a nominal victory for the Cavaliers.
29 October 1642	Charles I enters Oxford.
13 November 1642	Stand-off between armies of Charles I and Philip Skippon at Turnham Green. Charles withdraws to Oxford.
19 January 1643	Sir Ralph Hopton secures Cornwall for the King with his victory over Lord Ruthin at Braddock Down.
22 February 1643	Queen Henrietta Maria lands at Bridlington.
19 March 1643	Sir John Gell's Roundheads defeated by the Earl of Northampton's Cavaliers at Hopton Heath. Northampton is killed.
16 May 1643	Sir Ralph Hopton defeats the Earl of Stamford at Stratton.
18 June 1643	Prince Rupert victorious at Chalgrove Field. John Hampden is killed.
29 June 1643	Marquis of Newcastle defeats Lord Fairfax at Adwalton Moor.

A true and exact Relation of the
manner of his Maiesties setting up of His
Standard at *Nottingham*, on Munday the
22. of August 1642.

First, The forme of the Standard, as it is here figured, and who were present at the advancing of it

Secondly, The danger of setting up of former Standards, and the damage which ensued thereon.

Thirdly, A relation of all the Standards that ever were set up by any King.

Fourthly, the names of those Knights who are appointed to be the Kings Standard-bearers. With the forces that are appoynted to guard it.

Fifthly, The manner of the Kings comming first to *Coventry*.

Sixtly, The *Cavalieres* resolution and dangerous threats which they have uttered, if the King concludes a peace without them, or hearkens unto his great Councell the Parliament : Moreover how they have shared and divided *London* amongst themselves already.

London, printed for F. Coles. 1642,

The Raising of the King's Standard at Nottingham on 22 August 1642 was a time of confidence and optimism for Charles I. However, it was taken as an ill omen by some when the wind blew the standard over.

5 July 1643	The armies of Sir Ralph Hopton and Sir William Waller fight to a standstill at Lansdown.
13 July 1643	Hopton defeats Waller at Roundway Down.
26 July 1643	Prince Rupert takes Bristol.
28 July 1643	Sir John Meldrum defeats Cavaliers at Gainsborough. Sir Charles Cavendish is killed.
2 September 1643	Siege of Hull begins.
20 September 1643	Charles I defeated by the Earl of Essex at Newbury.
25 September 1643	Solemn League and Covenant between Parliament and the Scots.
11 October 1643	Sir William Widdrington defeated by the Earl of Manchester at Winceby.
12 October 1643	Newcastle abandons Siege of Hull.
19 January 1644	Scots Army invades England.
25 January 1644	Sir Thomas Fairfax defeats Lord Byron at Nantwich.
29 March 1644	Hopton defeated by Waller at Cheriton.
11 April 1644	Lord Fairfax defeats Bellasis at Selby.
22 April 1644	Siege of York begins.
29 June 1644	Charles I defeats Sir William Waller at Cropredy Bridge.
2 July 1644	Prince Rupert defeated at Marston Moor.
16 July 1644	Fall of York.
28 August 1644	Marquis of Montrose raises Charles I's standard in Scotland.
31 August 1644	Charles I defeats Earl of Essex at Lostwithiel.
1 September 1644	Montrose wins first victory over covenanters at Tippermuir.
27 October 1644	Charles I defeats Roundheads at 2nd Battle of Newbury.
2 April 1645	First units of New Model Army take the field.
9 May 1645	Montrose defeats Sir John Urry at Auldern.
14 June 1645	Charles I is defeated at Naseby.
2 July 1645	Montrose defeats General Baillie at Alford.
10 July 1645	Sir Thomas Fairfax defeats Lord Goring at Langport.

The topography of Marston Moor was unusual for a Civil War battlefield. As a rule, armies faced one another from the modest heights of gently rising ground which facilitated the movement of cavalry – as illustrated by the battlefields of Naseby (14 June 1645) and Langport (10 July 1645).

A non-partisan cartoon shows the opposing sides squaring up to one another. As the war progressed, propoganda became far more vitriolic. Is there any war, one wonders, in which the enemy has not been accused of murdering babes in arms?

15 August 1645	Montrose defeats Baillie at Kilsyth.
10 September 1645	Fall of Bristol.
13 September 1645	General Leslie defeats Montrose at Philiphaugh.
24 September 1645	Charles I defeated at Rowton Moor.
16/17 February 1646	Hopton defeated by Sir Thomas Fairfax at Torrington.
5 May 1646	Charles I surrenders to Scots at Southwell/End of First English Civil War.
3 September 1646	Marquis of Montrose leaves for Norway.
23 March 1648	Pembroke Castle declares for Charles I/ Second Civil War begins.
14 June 1648	Siege of Colchester begins.
17/18 August 1648	Cromwell defeats army of Scots and English Royalists at Preston.
28 August 1648	Surrender of Colchester/End of Second Civil War.
30 January 1649	Execution of King Charles I.
7 February 1649	Abolition of the monarchy.
23 March 1650	Montrose lands in the Orkneys/Third Civil War begins.
27 April 1650	Montrose defeated at Carbisdale.
21 May 1650	Execution of Montrose.
24 June 1650	Charles II lands at Garmouth.
3 September 1650	Cromwell defeats Scots at Dunbar.
1 January 1651	Charles II is crowned at Scone.
3 September 1651	Charles II is defeated at Worcester/Third Civil War ends.
16 December 1653	Inauguration of Oliver Cromwell as Lord Protector.

Appendices

FURTHER INFORMATION

Societies
The Cromwell Association
www.cromwell.argonet.uk
The Sealed Knot (Re-enactment Society)
www.sealedknot.org
The English Civil War Society (Re-enactment Society)
press@english-civil-war-society.org

Games
This Accursed Civil War (5 games including *Marston Moor*)
www.gmtgames.com
Marston Moor (World Wide Wargames)
www.secondchancegames.com

Film/Video
Cromwell (Feature Film 1970)
To Kill a King: Cromwell and Fairfax (Feature Film 2003)
Marston Moor (Factual) Cromwell Productions

CD-Rom
The English Civil War (Graphics/filmed recreations/text of
  Gardiner's Four Volume study of Civil Wars) Cromwell
  Productions (1997)

Websites
Searches for 'Marston Moor' and 'English Civil War' will uncover a
number of informative sites. Additional sites of interest, which
include admission information relating to buildings mentioned in the
text, are:
www.touruk.co.uk
www.ripleycastle.co.uk
www.english-heritage.org.uk
www.nationaltrust.org.uk
www.knaresborough.co.uk
www.caliverbooks.com
www.york.trust.museum
www.micklegatebar.co.uk
www.yas.org.uk
www.welcometoyork.co.uk
www.oldtykes.co.uk
www.battlefieldstrust.com
www.wakefield.gov.uk

Surviving Yorkshire Cavaliers were punished for their 'delinquencies' by being heavily fined. Sir William Ingilby of Ripley Castle was made to pay fines of £700 for a period of seven years. Ripley Castle

The Civil War Heritage of many buildings is now all but forgotten. Heslington Hall, now part of the University of York, may have been used by Lord Fairfax as his HQ during the siege of York. Three centuries later, in a very different war, it became the HQ of 4 Group Bomber Command.

ENGLISH CIVIL WAR SOCIETY

The King's Army

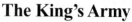

The Roundheads

We aim to bring this turbulent and exciting period of history to life, combining history, live action and public education. The Parliamentarian and King's forces have their own command structures which combine to offer both the spectacular and everyday activities of the 17th Century.

Our Living History displays portray social interaction, civil administration, food, clothing, entertainment complete with accurate reproduction of the artifacts of the time. Our members are practiced in military skills such as cavalry, pike, musket, sword, cannon and battlefield supply, and many are able to offer researched background about daily life, history and religion of the period.

What we can offer event organisers:
We can tailor events to your requirements and budget from carnivals and fetes to county fairs at schools, Heritage sites and show grounds, supporting educational projects, local historical events and as a major attraction at fund raising events. The number of participants and authentic equipment can be matched to the event from the tens to the many hundreds.

To join us or enquire about hosting an event please contact:

ECWS, 70 Hailgate, Howden, East Yorkshire DN14 7ST
Email: press@english-civil-war-society.org

The opportunity to take part in this exciting and rewarding hobby, learn the military and life skills of the time, take part in battle re-enactment and living histories, and join in the entertaining post event social activities, off-season training and banquets.

Ripley Castle
North Yorkshire

The splendour of a castle, the warmth of a family home

Visit the Castle and walled gardens, four acres of lawns, beds and borders. A pleasure to visit any time of the year.

Conferences at Ripley Castle
One of our most frequent tasks is to provide meeting facilities. From a handful of people, to top level Intergovernmental talks, the Castle takes everything calmly in its stride.

Corporate Entertaining
The Castle has been hosting private and corporate hospitality events for over twenty years, and we now cater for around 350 events each year.

Getting Married at Ripley Castle
When it comes to organising weddings, few venues can match our years of experience, professionalism, and ability to turn visions into reality.

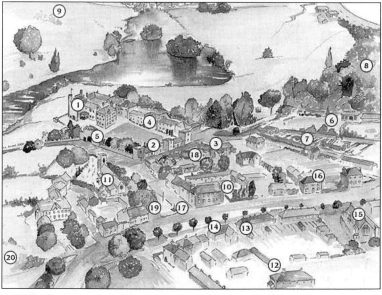

1. Ripley Castle
2. Gift Shop & toilets (inc. disabled and baby changing)
3. Castle Tearoom
4. East Wing
5. Gatehouse
6. Formal Walled Gardens
7. Kitchen Gardens
8. Pleasure Grounds
9. Deer park and lakeside walk
10. The Boar's Head Hotel and beer garden

11. All Saints' Church and Weeping Cross
12. Birchwood Farm Museum
13. Chantry House Art Gallery
14. Ripley Ice Creams and Village Stores
15. Hotel de Ville
16. Ripley Endowed School (1702)
17. Village Stocks
18. Hopkins Porter (Wine and Cheese)
19. Boar's Head drinking Fountain
20. Car Park and Public W.C.'s

Contact us: **The Ripley Castle Estate**
Harrogate, North Yorkshire HG3 3AY

Telephone : **01423 770152**
Fax : 01423 771745
Email: **enquiries@ripleycastle.co.uk**

Arms and armour of the English Civil Wars

on display at the Royal Armouries, Leeds

April-September:
Every day from
10.30 am to 5.30 pm

October-March:
Every day from
10 am to 4.30 pm

Royal Armouries Museum, Armouries Drive, LEEDS LS10 1LT
24 hour information: 08700 344 344   enquiries@armouries.org.uk

The Sealed Knot

English Civil War Re-enactment

Bringing the Past to Life...
...in Aid of the Future

History Comes Alive!

Why not go back in time to find out what life in the
17th Century was really like?

The Sealed Knot helps bring history alive every year at period
houses throughout the country where you can talk to major
historical figures, try out a few recipes, learn about the life of a
soldier on the march and maybe even 'take the King's shilling'.

What better way to teach children about the period than with a
little 'hands-on' experience.

The Sealed Knot has been heavily involved in education for many
years, giving school talks and displays about life in the Civil War
throughout the UK. If your school or college is running a project
on the Civil War period, *The Sealed Knot* can provide you with
experts on everything from cookery to clothes, education and
politics, through to weapons and battle strategies.

The Sealed Knot Ltd
Registered Office:
Equity Court
73-75 Millbrook Road East
Southampton, SO1 5RJ

The Sealed Knot Ltd
P.O. Box 2000
Nottingham
NG2 5LH
E-mail : info@sealedknot.org

INDEX

Italics entries refer to illustrations

174

David Clark visited his first battlefield (Stamford Bridge) in 1958 and has been researching British battlefields ever since. He currently teaches History at a sixth form college in Cambridge.